Working with YOUNG CHILDREN

THIRD EDITION

JENNIE LINDON

Hodder & Stoughton

A MEMBER OF THE HODDER HEADLINE GROUP

To my parents who, with their love and their pleasure in children,
have taught me volumes.

BIOGRAPHICAL NOTE

Jennie Lindon (B.A., M.Phil., C.Psychol.) is a Chartered Psychologist who has specialised in services for children and their families. She has written extensively for those who work with children, young people and their families. She has also published books and articles written for parents and their concerns within the family.

British Library Cataloguing in Publication Data

ISBN 0 340 68802 5

A catalogue entry for this title is available from the British Library.

First published 1997
Impression number   10   9   8   7   6   5   4   3   2   1
Year   2000   1999   1998   1997

Typeset by Wearset, Boldon, Tyne and Wear.
Printed in Great Britain for Hodder & Stoughton Educational, a division of Hodder Headline Plc, 338 Euston Road, London NW1 3Bh by Scotprint Ltd, Musselburgh, Scotland

CONTENTS

ACKNOWLEDGEMENTS

Many thanks to Lance Lindon who took all the photographs and to the staff, parents and children who appear in them – from the Balham Family Centre and Balham Leisure Centre crèche.

How I work and write still owes a debt to people whom I thanked in the early editions of this book. So I would like to repeat my appreciation of discussions with William Mitchell, Tim Smithells, Michael Stanton and Helen Wilson. I continue to enjoy learning from early years workers in different settings and from colleagues who work in early years, with particular thanks to the Early Childhood Unit of the National Children's Bureau.

I no longer need to thank someone who has cared for my children while I work, since they are now a very capable fourteen and sixteen years old. So, I am going to thank Drew and Tanith themselves for the great pleasure they have brought me and how much I have learned from being with them. (For anyone who is comparing different editions of this book, I would add that I have not swapped my daughter. She decided in nursery school to be known by her second name and no longer as Zoe.)

INTRODUCTION

The first edition of *Working with Young Children* was published in 1983 and the extended, second edition in 1987. I have been very pleased to have the opportunity to revise that edition in the second half of the 1990s. The task of deciding how the book should be modified has highlighted in the ways which the early years field has changed since the early 1980s.

Observation and assessment

Early years workers have become considerably more aware of the importance of observing children and of keeping informative records. There are many views on how best to undertake this work, not least with the influence of the National Curriculum extending into early years. But there no longer is the need of the 1980s to make a persuasive case that workers should organise themselves to make focused observations.

Equal opportunities

The 1980s showed that indirect approaches to changing practice over equal opportunities were really not working. Since then, development of policy and attention to key principles have become far more direct. The application of principle to practice has been focused not only on removing inequalities, whether intentional or not, but also to promoting an active anti-bias approach through all aspects of daily running, the early years curriculum and relationships with parents.

I still hold the view that equal opportunities – on ethnic group and culture, gender and disabilities – needs to be an integral part of practice and not a separate issue. So you will not find a new section but I have made modifications throughout the text.

Partnership with parents

Since the early 1980s the whole idea of working with parents in a far more equal way has developed tremendously. Undoubtedly, in some areas of the early years services there is still much to be done with workers or whole groups who are not welcoming to parents and other carers. However, rather like the material on observation, I have become aware that I no longer have to take the persuasive stance of my previous Part 4.

Learning – early years curriculum

Part 3 has been shifted in emphasis towards learning as a whole, rather than language development. The content has been modified to acknowledge the changes towards an early years curriculum. This whole area of work is in a state of development and flux, with some workers anxious about the curriculum approach, partly because of uneasiness about assessment focused on individual children.

Behaviour and whole behaviour policies

I have not changed my views about a positive approach to children's behaviour and the importance of adults' looking at their own actions. During the 1980s and 1990s many early years centres have taken a serious, overall look at how they handle children's behaviour, the real messages that children read from adults' behaviour and the importance of communication with parents. For some centres and schools this has resulted in a public policy on behaviour.

In conclusion

Some of the examples and case studies have been developed from those in the earlier edition but many new ones have been added. All have been based on real people and places. But names and other details have always been changed to maintain confidentiality.

The changes in the book do not negate the approaches that I believed to be practical and sensible when I wrote the first and second editions. The early years field has moved on, in many ways very positively, and any book has to reflect how issues are discussed now. I still feel equally strongly about children's well-being, their learning and happiness. Children have not changed in the intervening years but concerns about how best to work with them in early childhood have evolved and the changes in this edition reflect those developments.

PART 1

OBSERVATION, PLANNING AND RECORD KEEPING

1

GOOD PRACTICE IN OBSERVATION AND PLANNING

A PLANNED APPROACH

Within any early years setting you will need careful discussion about what kinds of observation will be most valuable and how you will record your observations. But, equally important, will be the conversations you have with colleagues and parents about what can be learned from the observations. You do not simply want to create a pile of paperwork.

You need an overview of your efforts with children if your work is to be effective.

- Without a guiding framework you may make observations on children that never seem to be blended with daily practice. The observations are interesting but where do they lead you?
- It is also possible that you may work hard with individual children or a small group with similar needs and underestimate how much progress you have made. Your perceptions of children are grounded in the present, and that is sensible, but you also need a check on how they have changed since the recent and not so recent past. You may have forgotten how much this group was struggling two months ago.
- Clear plans will also support good communication with parents because you can share what you are doing and why. You will increase the chances that parents are interested and motivated to make useful links to what they do with children at home.
- A planned approach can highlight what you have managed with children, sometimes with the enthusiastic cooperation of their parents. You will also be more realistic about how much more is yet to be done with some children. Overall your work can be more satisfying as well as more effective.

The diagram on page 4 summarises the main elements in this planned approach.

Settling a child into the group

When a child arrives in any early years setting, you will gather some background information. Good practice is to set up an individual record with details about the child, her family and individual needs. If you work in a children's or family centre you may take referrals from health visitors or social workers. In this case, some further background information may come in the form of a report. The details can be helpful but you will

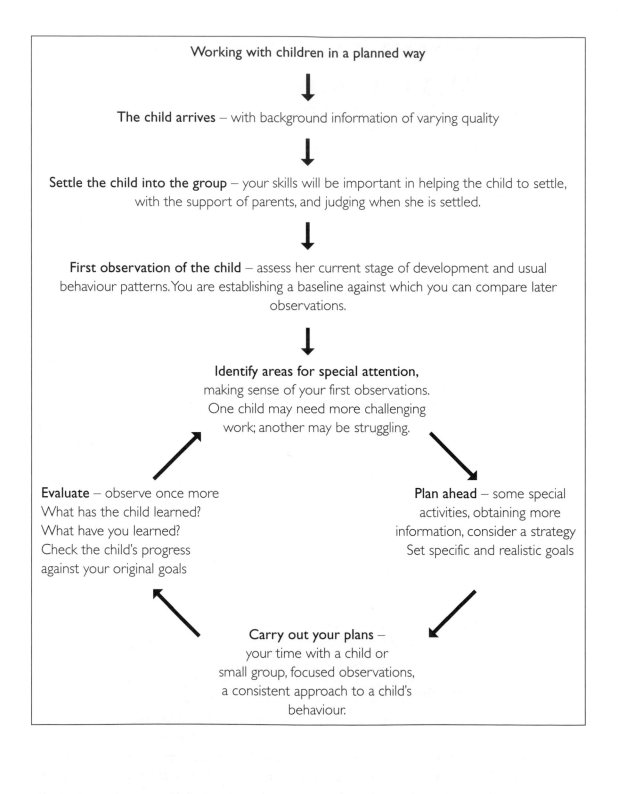

Working with children in a planned way

↓

The child arrives – with background information of varying quality

↓

Settle the child into the group – your skills will be important in helping the child to settle, with the support of parents, and judging when she is settled.

↓

First observation of the child – assess her current stage of development and usual behaviour patterns. You are establishing a baseline against which you can compare later observations.

↓

Identify areas for special attention,
making sense of your first observations.
One child may need more challenging
work; another may be struggling.

Evaluate – observe once more
What has the child learned?
What have you learned?
Check the child's progress
against your original goals

Plan ahead – some special
activities, obtaining more
information, consider a strategy
Set specific and realistic goals

Carry out your plans –
your time with a child or
small group, focused observations,
a consistent approach to a child's
behaviour.

need to make your own working relationship with parents and friendly, personal contact with the children.

You may make brief notes in the early weeks of settling, since you will then have a later reminder of how this child coped with a new setting and people. The early days will also be a good time to talk with the parent or other carer who settles the child. You can share your notes and explain in a positive way how observations work in your setting.

The first organised observation

A reliable observation of children's abilities, interests and usual behaviour must wait until they are settled. A first stage of settling will be when the child is happy, or reasonably happy, to let her parent or carer leave. However, it may be several weeks before some children appear at ease in your setting and look fairly confident as they choose play activities, make contact with other children and approach workers. When you judge this point has been reached it makes sense to time your first organised observation of a child, which will provide your comparison point with later observations.

Different settings work with a variety of record sheets and guides to observation. Chapter 2 covers some of the possibilities but the approach described here is applicable whatever the exact approach taken to observation in your centre.

If you work in the reception class of a primary school then you will be involved in the baseline assessment proposed as the first step in the National Curriculum assessment process. At the time of writing (1996) the details of this initial assessment of children were not final, but the possible schemes of baseline observation would be compatible with the planning approach discussed in this chapter.

A positive focus

The aim of observation and the record that you write up is to guide you in identifying areas in which your attention, and that of your colleagues, could be best focused for this individual child. Some highlights might be:

- Four-year-old Martha is progressing well in all aspects of her development. Although you do not usually start reading with the children in the centre, Martha is ready and wants to learn. If anything, she shows signs of mild mischief-making from boredom.
- You are concerned about Greg. Nearly three-and-a-half, his language is more like that of a two-year-old. He is physically confident, even bold, but has a lot of minor accidents. He has trouble with fine coordinations and does not look or listen with care.
- Three-year-old Carline has physical disabilities that affect her mobility and some hearing loss. You were uneasy about the reaction from other children, since she is the only child with disabilities in the group. However, her father helped to settle Carline

and dealt factually with questions from other children. Carline has made friends and the other children make friendly allowances for her mobility needs. Her father is pleased to share ideas on communication from the learning programme that they are using with Carline at home.

Planning activities with children

Within the centre you should have plans for the whole group, most likely built into the framework of an early years curriculum (see Chapter 6). However, any overall plans have to be tailored for individual children.

- You might plan some specific activities for a child whose development concerns you or a small group who are experiencing similar difficulties. When you are concerned about a child, it can be tempting to try more of everything, but a focused approach is far more likely to help.
- A child like Martha (see page 5) may need some specific attention and more challenging activities than many of her peers, if she is not to be tempted into mildly disruptive behaviour because she is not being stretched.
- Sometimes your plans may be less about specific activities than being alert to drawing a child into a group of other children, perhaps supporting a child who has difficulty in joining and playing with other children.

Special activities
Children whose development is delayed or who have other special needs, for instance difficulties in attention, will benefit from specifically chosen activities. You will need to consider what kind of activity is most likely to interest the child and be appropriate to her current abilities and attention span. Creative ideas will not help if the activities are pitched at too complex a level, require a level of concentration that is currently beyond this child or which mean you waste precious time coaxing her into activities that she does not enjoy.

For example:

Four-year-old Max has great difficulty using scissors in any craft activity. His friends are coping well and Max is becoming self-conscious about asking for help. Max's key worker, Amy, has noticed his difficulties but does not plan special attention built only around learning to cut with scissors. Amy has observed that Max also lacks confidence in other fine coordinations and often looks uncertain when trying to build with small pieces or lining up beads for threading. So, Amy plans to help Max with wielding the scissors but also to support him in holding, looking carefully and using small tools in a range of play activities.

Distinction between special activities and observations
Planning any special activities is separate from observation and assessment of children's current abilities. The observations, and any developmental record form, will give you guidance for planning, but these do not form the precise plans of what you now do with children. You definitely do not focus any special attention exclusively on particular items in a developmental record form or only one small area in an observation schedule.

Planning to find more information
Your immediate plans for an individual child will not always be play activities in which you become involved with the child. Sometimes, your careful observation will have pointed to a gap in your working knowledge of the child. You might seek further information in a number of ways:

● Talk with your colleagues about what they have noticed about this child.
● Have a conversation with the child's parents, perhaps asking them some specific questions.
● Plan an additional and specific observation of the child. For example: three and a half year old James is frequently told off for hurting other children. You are aware of the risk that James is getting a name for himself as a 'naughty child' and you want to gather information on his behaviour with a view to managing incidents more positively.
● After consulting with the parents, seek a specialist test for the child. Perhaps both you and her parents suspect that two-year-old Ramona has some visual loss. You have all watched her carefully and agree that Ramona holds books and small toys very close to her face. Even allowing for her age, she seems not to notice some events in the nursery, especially those that occur to the side of her. Ramona's parents are happy for you to find out where they can go to seek a full assessment of Ramona's vision.

For example:

Amy is aware of Max's current difficulties in fine physical coordinations. But she would like more information on what exactly Max is finding difficult, so that she could plan her support at the best level and in the most helpful way. Amy decides to watch Max carefully over the next week to identify to what extent the difficulties may be related to how Max holds items, whether he is looking carefully and his general level of physical competence.

Set clear goals

Part of your planning, either specific activities with a child or additional observations, is to set specific and realistic goals.

Goals need to be specific so that you do not spend time and energy, possibly involving parents as well, on a vague plan to 'stretch Martha more in the playgroup'. Vague goals will also leave you dissatisfied because it will be far harder to judge what kind of progress or changes have happened after your special efforts.

You are far more likely to be able to set definite goals if your thinking has been properly focused at the step of identifying what needs your attention. Perhaps you have left your concern about a child as a vague description such as 'Max seems clumsy' or 'Greg really ought to be talking properly by now'.

To be effective you need to be able to pinpoint, with as much descriptive detail as possible, what a child can currently manage and therefore where the special attention from adults could most sensibly be directed. If a child is seen as 'slow', then what is it about her play and behaviour that leads adults to this judgement? Does she seem to be delayed in most areas of her development and, if so, to what extent? If a child is seen to have 'poor concentration', then what does this mean? For how long does he usually concentrate and are there some activities that hold his interest for longer than others?

Goals are the means to be concrete and positive about those changes you would like to see in a child and towards which you are working. If you judge that further observation would help, then your goals will be set in terms of exactly what you want to learn about this child's development or behaviour. If you are planning some special activities or sessions, then your goal will be a clear description, although brief, of the change you would like to see in the child – what she will have learned or how her behaviour will have changed.

As well as being specific, your goals should also be realistic. It is very disheartening for workers, and parents who become involved in special work, if they have set too large a step, given the child's current abilities. In the given time period, there will appear to be very little change, but it was unlikely that the child would learn or change that fast.

Keeping notes

It is good practice to keep descriptive notes of your observations, goals and work with children and to share these with parents. You could organise planning notes around these three headings:

1 What is your focus? It may be a problem, or an area of concern, but could also be the sense that a child is capable of much more than she currently shows.
2 Exactly what would you like to achieve with this child in the near future. Think no more than a few weeks ahead. Be specific and realistic in the detail of these plans and describe the child – her abilities and behaviour, not play activities (these are point 3).

3 What activities will you undertake as special work with this child? Or how will you use the existing play curriculum? If you are ready for a plan of activities then select them in the light of this child's interests and abilities. If you need more information, what exactly are you missing at the moment, and what would be useful to discover?

There will be variations in the way that activities are run with children. One child may be unable to concentrate with any distractions and so may only benefit from structured, one-to-one sessions with her key worker. Other children may manage well in a small group with peers who are at a similar developmental level. The length of any special sessions have to be tailored to a child's ability and attention span. Children whose ability to concentrate is very limited may benefit from short bursts of attention from their key worker and encouragement to finish simple tasks. As their attention improves, they could be involved in longer play sessions or might be encouraged to try a new activity that needs greater perseverance.

The keynote is flexibility. It will definitely be more effective to organise yourself to have shorter but more frequent sessions with a child than to hope to spend long sessions, with unrealistic implications for staff organisation so that your plans are disrupted. From the child's point of view, short and frequent sessions will provide more continuity and support learning far better than longer sessions with lengthy gaps in between.

Carry out your plans
This is sometimes the point at which the planned approach to working with children can break down. The plans may have been made with care and you, and perhaps the child's parent, who is motivated to work with you, are pleased to have a positive strategy for the child's behaviour or a definite focus for his language difficulties. Then, unforeseen events upset the plans. Perhaps the child is absent because of sickness, or a crisis in the centre means that special sessions have to be re-scheduled. However realistic you have tried to be, perhaps you, your colleagues or the child's parent were expecting that a fresh approach would make a significant difference very quickly and adults become disheartened. Sometimes you may find that colleagues do not support you in the way you asked.

It is at this stage that you will appreciate and need support from colleagues to persevere despite the difficulties, or at least allow your plans a fair chance before re-thinking them. Sometimes you will find support from a child's parent when you have developed a friendly working relationship.

Achievement of goals
Part of your plans was a clear description of the goal or goals you wanted to achieve with this child within a realistic period of time. You now need to check whether, or to what extent, you have reached those goals. For instance:

- If you made a more detailed observation, sought information from someone else or arranged a specialist assessment, have these activities provided useful information – answered the questions you asked?
- If you were carrying out special sessions to help a child's development, has that child made the progress you hoped?
- If your concern was that the curriculum was not stretching a child's abilities have you now found ways to give him or her a more satisfying challenge within the ordinary day?

Where you have given special attention for a developmental difficulty or delay, you may now judge that the child will be more able to make use of the usual nursery or playgroup activities. Special sessions may stop but it will be important that regular observation helps you to keep track of the child's progress. You need also to be aware that children often like special sessions and may be sad when they end. Be careful that you are still paying plenty of attention to what the child does and achieves through her play. Attention you give to children within the normal day may not be so obviously different when you shift from time spent to help with a problem to time that is guided by a child's immediate interests.

When children are experiencing several difficulties you will move from being pleased over the achievement of one goal towards setting a new goal. Perhaps a child's ability to concentrate has improved to the point that you can now sensibly plan activities focused on her language delay, or judge that she could now manage to join the special language support group.

When children are significantly delayed in their development then your long-term plans for them will have included many smaller goals. The achievement of each goal along the route will be an achievement to be celebrated with children and their parents. The same step-wise approach is a positive way forward in working with children with disabilities. The Portage programme, for instance, helps workers and parents to identify small enough steps to experience a sense of progress. Some children have severe learning disabilities that affect most of their development, whereas other children may experience difficulties and frustrations particularly in one or two areas of development most affected by a disability.

So, for some children, your work will circle again and again around the diagram on page 4 as you develop the next plan. Other children may not need this kind of focused attention after some time. Yet a regular check on all the children will be the way to ensure that difficulties are not developing unnoticed. The same pattern of alertness and regular assessment can be a source of satisfaction to workers and parents as well as a reminder when children are ready for new and different challenges in their play through the curriculum.

CASE STUDIES

Three longer case studies follow which illustrate that events often do not run smoothly in any early years setting, but that perseverance and a willingness to focus on any progress can lead to satisfying results.

One: Susan

Susan was nearly four years old and attended Boundaries playgroup for half-day sessions. The centre used a developmental record booklet as a means of regular assessment and Susan's progress was fine for her age. However, all the centre staff admitted to becoming very irritated with Susan's behaviour. She seemed to delight in being uncooperative, would do the exact opposite of what she was asked and was very cheeky to staff.

None of the staff wanted this situation to continue and they gave time to discussing Susan's behaviour in a team meeting. The staff most involved with Susan felt that she might be competing for attention in the only way she knew. Susan's family ran the local shop and seemed to be busy much of the time. Susan's play experience had been very limited and she seemed to view adults as unpredictable and unlikely to give her attention.

Marion, Susan's key worker, developed two goals that she wanted to achieve within 2–3 weeks.

1 To discourage Susan from trying for attention through cheeky or uncooperative behaviour. Marion decided to use the strategy of, as far as possible, ignoring Susan on these occasions and making herself available whenever Susan was cooperative and trying to play.
2 To interest Susan in play activities suitable for her age. Drawing was chosen as something in which Susan had shown interest. The aims were to extend Susan's skills and to encourage her to see adults as a useful resource.

Susan attended every morning session and reacted with enthusiasm to the structured attention from Marion. Within a fortnight there was an improvement in Susan's behaviour that was noticed by all the staff. She was far more cooperative and her cheekiness now seemed to be more in fun than a desire to provoke. Susan clearly enjoyed her special drawing sessions and was proud of what she had produced. She wanted to have conversations with staff, listening as well as making her own contribution.

Marion had developed a friendly relationship with Susan's mother who told her how Susan had talked at home about what she had done at nursery. She wanted to involve her parents in similar play activities at home – not only the drawing. Her parents had enjoyed this shift and seemed relieved that Susan was asking for their attention in non-irritating ways. Susan's mother explained to Marion how she and her husband made more efforts to play with Susan and were giving her little jobs to do when they were serving in the shop.

Marion felt that Susan did not need special sessions any more and aimed to continue to interest her in a wider range of play activities and to meet Susan's reasonable need for attention through play and conversation.

Comments and questions:

It would have been all too easy for staff to be irritated by Susan's behaviour and not to look for any positives.

- Are you working with children for whom you need to find a positive focus, as Marion did with Susan?
- Are you willing to look at your feelings as a source of information about a situation with a child but not as the final definition of what is happening? How might the child be feeling and making sense of the situation?
- In this example, a friendly relationship developed with a parent and changes happened at home as well as in the centre. Are you perhaps working with some parents who really have very few ideas about how to play with their children or that time spent in some play might make life generally more enjoyable?

Two: Yusif

Yusif was just over three years old when he was referred to Downview specialist playgroup. By nature of the referrals, the playgroup was becoming a setting to support children in becoming bilingual and ran a special language group. Yusif's attendance was very irregular and it was two months before his key worker, Annie, felt that she had some sense of his usual behaviour. In consultation with colleagues, Annie decided that Yusif was experiencing social difficulties within the playgroup, that needed to be tackled before any special language support. The two main issues were:

1 Yusif did not yet seem to have the social skills to join a group. He tended to hover on the outside but when he did approach a group of children his tactics tended to be aggressive, pushing the others or snatching their play materials.
2 Most of the play materials seemed unfamiliar to Yusif. For instance, his response to play dough was to hit it rather than make anything and his difficulties in

settling into an activity group meant that he did not stay long enough to see how other children were playing with the materials.

Annie set herself the goal that at least once every day she would draw Yusif into a small group of children who were absorbed in an activity and encourage him to sit beside her. She had noticed that Yusif tended to stay a little longer in a group when an adult was present. The other advantage was that she could stop the poking and prodding that seemed to be Yusif's only way of making contact with the other children, and hopefully make space for less disruptive overtures. Annie's aim was that in 2–3 weeks, Yusif would have gained the confidence and social skills to join a group without having to be coaxed and would stay at least some minutes.

Unfortunately, Yusif's pattern of irregular attendance continued. Annie had difficulty communicating with his mother since they did not share a language and the playgroup was unable to arrange an interpreter. Attempts over the next two months to draw Yusif into small group activities were interrupted by days, sometimes a week, of absence. Annie became very disheartened, however her colleagues were able to reassure her that, although slow, they could see changes in Yusif's reactions to the playgroup setting. Other staff could give examples of times that Yusif had joined a group of his own accord and without using his more aggressive tactics to gain entry. After ten weeks of irregular attendance another organised observation showed that Yusif was able to attend to and understand simple suggestions about his immediate play. He also used a small number of English words spontaneously. At this point Annie decided that Yusif was likely to benefit in the language group.

Comments and questions:

Irregular attendance can disturb the continuity when you are offering help to a child, but it may be unrealistic to postpone help for a regular pattern that is unlikely to emerge.

- Are you working with children who attend irregularly? How is this affecting your work?
- Is it possible to talk with their parents and communicate just how much more could be possible if the child used the place to the full? What might you say?
- If there is no easy way through to parents, how might you adjust your plans to take realistic account of the situation?
- Look at how you and your colleagues offer each other support when there is a risk of becoming disheartened in your work with children.

Three: Julie

Julie had experienced many changes in her life and had attended several different local authority nurseries and spent some time in residential care. When she was four and a half years old the nursery she was attending closed down and she made another move, to Edward Road Nursery.

Within a few weeks Julie had become a serious concern for staff because of her frequent and severe temper tantrums. The two staff responsible for the group, Mary and Barbara, observed that Julie lost her temper over almost any frustration: not having a worker's attention immediately, sharing play materials with another child or being thwarted over forbidden activities (such as climbing the fence). When she went into a tantrum, Julie would cry and scream, attack adults or other children, throw things and be very hard to control and comfort. An observation check over two weeks showed that she was having at least one tantrum, often serious, each day and the other children were showing signs of distress and fear.

Mary and Barbara recognised that much of Julie's behaviour came from the many changes she had experienced but they had also seen that any attempts to make allowances for her tended to be seen as a sign of weakness and Julie pushed anyone's patience to the very limits. Mary and Barbara agreed that their goal was to reduce the number of Julie's tantrums and they agreed a strategy that included:

- Clear limits on what Julie was and was not allowed to do, including the point at which one of them would intervene. They used time-out when Julie lost her temper, putting her in the corner of the room or sometimes outside to allow her to cool down.
- Allowing Julie the kind of activities that were normal for four-year-olds in the nursery, such as helping out and accompanying staff on local trips. This was a brave decision since Julie had to be constantly watched, since she would dash off without warning.
- Wherever possible, Mary and Barbara attempted to distract Julie from going into a tantrum. They used incentives to encourage good behaviour and made every effort to be encouraging for any positive behaviour from Julie.

Mary and Barbara made great efforts to be both consistent, patient and affectionate towards Julie. Julie's tantrums were somewhat reduced and she became easier to comfort. However, internal conflict in this nursery had led to a poor working atmosphere and other staff were loath to follow the strategies agreed by Mary and Barbara. The consequence was that Julie was treated in unpredictable ways by other staff in the nursery's garden area and a senior staff member sometimes removed Julie from the time-out situation, against the room staff's request.

Mary and Barbara supported each other in focusing on any positive developments and also started special projects for Julie, supported by weekly play sessions given by a visiting Educational Psychologist. The aim was to stretch Julie's abilities and prepare her for school. She clearly enjoyed the special sessions but usually threw a tantrum when she had to return to the main group of children.

The difficulties experienced by Julie were not solved before she left the nursery for school. Mary and Barbara put in a great deal of effort but would probably have achieved far more with a greater length of time with Julie and cooperation from their colleagues.

Comments and questions

- Julie was an unhappy child whose behaviour would have been hard for anyone to handle. How have you dealt with similar situations?
- Inconsistency between staff was an additional problem in this example. How might a poor working atmosphere be tackled?
- In difficult situations it can be important for everyone's well being to focus on the positives, even if these seem to be few. Do you have situations like this that you are facing at the moment? Take some time to list the positives rather than focus exclusively on the negatives.

GOOD PRACTICE IN WRITING REPORTS

Observations of any kind should be written up. There needs to be sufficient detail that you or a colleague, reading the notes later, can understand what was observed and the practical conclusions drawn. On the other hand you do not want pages and pages of detail in which the main points are buried. More useful reports tend to emerge when centres have ready-prepared sheets with appropriate headings for the different kinds of observations and other reports on children. Part of the role of the senior workers is also to support and supervise less experienced colleagues in their report writing.

Sharing reports with parents

Good practice is that parents should have straightforward access to any records on their own children. This guideline applies in early years education and care, medical services and playwork. Legal requirements underpin good practice. For instance, the Data Protection Act 1984 obliges anyone who keeps personal records on computer to make them available to those people. The Access to Personal Files Act 1987 extended this obligation to manual records held by local authorities and the Access to Health Records Act 1990 to medical records written after November 1991.

Access may work differently in the varied settings and some parents will still find that their request to see their child's records is followed by delays or a less than welcome approach to making the records available. It is still the case that workers can only make accessible the material from their own centre or immediate service. Third party information has to be removed from a record before parents are allowed to read it. However, some local authorities have as written policy that reports and letters about children go on open record unless the relevant professional specifies otherwise.

Parents were not always allowed access to their children's records. Open access has been part of a more general social concern about the rights of anyone to read personal material and parents are responsible for their children. There are a number of pressing reasons why parents should have easy access to their children's records.

- Parents have long-term responsibility for the well-being of their children. They have the right to know the perspectives and opinions of other adults who *temporarily* share that responsibility.
- The majority of parents are very interested in their own children and want to know how they are behaving and progressing out of the home.
- When records are open and easily available to parents it increases the possibility of exchange of information, views and ideas between workers and parents. You can learn from each other.
- It is possible that a child's record may have factual errors that a parent can correct. For example, it is not unknown for a mistake to be made in a child's date of birth.
- When it was more usual for files to be closed to parents, there were undoubtedly instances when professionals wrote unsupported opinions as if they were facts. Such myths then often travelled on with the families who were unaware of the claims in their files. Unprofessional, offhand remarks were also written in the file which would not have been expressed to the parent face-to-face.
- The very existence of closed files, or a complex way of gaining access, makes parents feel rejected from this part of their child's life. They are also likely to be suspicious, perhaps with reason, that uncomplimentary material is contained in the file.

Previous resistance to having open files and any current anxiety in staff groups tends to cluster around claims that records and reports cannot be honest and that parents will be annoyed by what they read. Undoubtedly, a minority of parents are prone to anger, but they will find a focus regardless of your policy on records. Some professionals still claim that parents will not understand the content of reports or records. This negative outlook is not justified by the reactions of most parents. Usually parents are interested, want to know more and are encouraged towards conversation with staff, which increase the chance of continuity between home and early years settings.

Communication with parents is part of good practice.

Writing positive and honest reports

The move towards sharing written material has almost certainly changed how reports and records are written. Most of this change has been in the direction of better practice. It will not be useful for a child if you feel obliged to be tactful to the point of saying nothing of substance in a report. You do need to think about how you write and support your comments. For reports to be useful to parents the information must be given in such a way that parents can understand the written material, are able to accept the information and can do something about what they read (or hear in conversation with you).

The following practical suggestions should guide any report writing, regardless of who will read the finished report.

Straightforward language

Most professions have a shared language and some words or phrases are used so often that it is easy to forget that the rest of the adult world does not talk in this way. If your centre has created a welcoming atmosphere for parents they may feel comfortable to ask, 'What do you mean by that?' but it is better for written material to be written in plain English in the first place.

Some parents whose first language is not English may be fully fluent in written and spoken English but some will not. Good practice will be to have a conversation that supplements any written reports and to seek an interpreter where possible. Realistically, interpretation facilities may not be easily available or the service may involve a fee and your centre cannot pay for more than a small number of sessions. Sometimes a bilingual colleague may be able to help or, if the parent is willing, then another parent or friend might help with clear communication, although undoubtedly conversations can go astray if you can speak none of the other language.

Putting opinions in their rightful place

The opinions of a worker spending time with a child are valuable, because they are rooted in knowledge of that individual child and a broader base of knowledge of children of a similar age. However, opinions must be presented honestly and not as universally agreed facts. Sometimes you should be writing 'I think that . . .', 'I am concerned that . . .' or 'I am pleased that . . .'. Any worker should be ready to sign and date a report or notes. If you are not prepared to take personal responsibility for what you have written, expecting that parents will read it, then it is questionable whether you should be writing it at all.

A sound rule of thumb is never to write down a comment that you would be embarrassed for another adult to read – or for the child to read if you work with older children. Of course, you do not therefore avoid writing down notes about any upsetting incident or activities that did not go as well as a colleague expected. Such censored notes would be of little use to anyone. Appropriate caution is that no worker should jot down offhand remarks or unsupported opinions. For instance:

- There is a world of difference between writing the judgement of 'The collage activity was a failure' and the descriptive comment of 'The children appeared to lose interest in the collage snowman activity. Possibly the areas that had to be stuck with cotton wool were too large and led to repetition'.
- Even if you feel you have observed poor practice, you are far more likely to have a fruitful discussion based on your notes if you avoid blunt judgements. For instance, of the following two written comments which is more likely to lead to a discussion about whether 'we as a staff group are attentive enough to the children'?
    i 'Andrea called twice to worker (Natalie). N. talking with two other staff. A. looked for a while then walked off.'

ii 'Andrea called to Natalie. N. too busy chatting with two other staff to bother.'

Support your opinions
You need to explain how you have reached a particular opinion. You are not building up a defence case but are sharing your observations and how you have considered them. Sometimes you may feel uncertain, you have a 'gut feeling'. Then it is your responsibility to identify the sources of this feeling, which may well be accurate but have to be supported. Sometimes you may be able to give shape to a vague worry through discussion with a colleague.

When parents are allowed to follow how you have reached an opinion, then discussion is possible. Parents' experience of their child will be different and they should be given the chance to express a different opinion to yours, perhaps to add a written comment of their own.

When you take responsibility for your opinions and support them, then you will avoid blunt and unhelpful judgements about children or their parents. Workers are usually more worried about parents' reaction to critical comments. However, unsupported positive remarks are not very useful in the long run. It may seem pleasant for a parent to read that, 'Shahana is a bright little girl'. Yet, without the supporting evidence, nobody can tell whether this brief opinion is a sound description of Shahana or an empty compliment.

Focus on what you have observed
You need to remain specific to what you have experienced of a child and not generalise further – either in a positive or negative way. You will observe and can comment on children's behaviour when they are with you, but this does not give you a sound basis to generalise on their personality. (This point is taken up again on page 136 about a positive approach to children's behaviour.) Nor can you assume that children will behave in the same way in other settings. In fact children are often responsive to differences in adult behaviour and this is reflected in their own reactions. For example:

- It is more appropriate to write (or to say in discussion) that 'Jamie seems much shorter on patience in the mornings' than to generalise to a criticism that 'Jamie is a short-tempered boy'.
- It sounds like a friendly compliment to write or say that 'Debbie is always such a helpful child'. But perhaps Debbie is very different at home and gives her mother a hard time. Specific comments will be more accurate and perhaps help Debbie's mother to look for changes at home. You might write as an alternative, 'Debbie seems to bloom with responsibility and when I ask her to help. She is a great finder of lost pieces of jigsaw and can be trusted to take messages within the nursery.'

Describe rather than blame
You may have opinions about what is making matters worse or better for an individual

child but you cannot be certain. Where you judge there is a problem you may be tempted to find fault – with a colleague or the parents. However, if you express this in a blaming way, then you are most likely to encourage your colleague or the parent to blame you in return.

You will have a much better chance of a useful conversation if you comment (in a descriptive way) that, 'Damian seems to settle better on those days when his mother can stay with him for a short while'. In contrast, a comment like, 'Damian is upset because his Mum will not stay to settle him' is placing direct blame on his mother, who may have her own reasons for hurrying away on some days.

Be provisional

Yours is one opinion among many and you should allow space for other possibilities. You may be experienced but nobody is a 100% expert; you could be wrong or not know some items of information. There will always be some aspects of a child's life about which you are ignorant. It is far better to write (or say), 'Perhaps Sandy needs more. . . .' or 'I think it would help Winston if . . .' rather than, 'Sandy's problem is obviously that . . .' or 'If only Winston had . . . then . . .'.

Equality with parents

Both you and a child's parents bring different packages of knowledge and expertise to your conversation about a child. You need to respect, although you will not necessarily agree with, each other's views. What you write should acknowledge that your observations are only in the one setting. What works well for you in the nursery or playgroup may work at home, or it may not, since home is a different setting. Reports should acknowledge that parents have an understanding of their own child and could contribute to the understanding of the centre.

You might write in a child's file, 'Abigail often gets upset when I suggest she tries something in a different way. Note to discuss with her parents whether Abigail is like this at home'. The results of your experience with a child, and what you have noted in his record, can be shared in a courteous way in conversation with parents. For instance, 'I've found that if I stick to what I've told Andy to do, he stops arguing fairly soon. But I've also learned to let the minor things go. What do you find works best at home?'

Focus on what is happening

It is better to focus the detail of your report on your observations on what happens and to be tentative rather than to reach firm conclusions about why. Possible reasons may well emerge through discussion about an individual child – with your colleague or the child's parent.

For instance, in conversation with parents, 'Why doesn't Michelle pay attention?' is likely to put them on the defensive. Alternatively, 'What do you find best to get Michelle to pay attention?' focuses on behaviour and asks parents for their expertise.

Other positive starters are 'What sense do you make of it when Thomas . . .?' or 'What do you think is going through Erin's mind when she . . .?' These questions ask for description, step aside from any issues of blame and recognise that parents have ideas to contribute.

A good standard in reports

Good practice in report writing is not different depending on whether or not parents will read what you have written. The guidelines above hold for any report. From the same starting point of your observations and accumulated knowledge of an individual child, you can give a more or less constructive message to parents. There is no certain formula to ensure that parents will never be upset or confused by your written comments or what you say in conversation. These practical guidelines will, however, increase the chances that you make helpful comments that lead to sharing ideas rather than argument.

2

OBSERVATION AND ASSESSMENT OF CHILDREN'S PROGRESS

Even experienced early years workers need to make regular observations of the children for whom they are responsible. It simply is not possible to notice and remember everything and, at the same time, to offer children a rounded experience of play and learning in the setting. Three elements combine in good practice with children:

- Regular observation in addition to the effort to remain alert to what is happening daily in the group. Observation has a focus if it is to be most useful and requires the concentrated use of your senses – mainly looking and listening.
- Assessment is made on the basis of observation, blended with other sources of information, including parents' input. Assessment inevitably involves some judgement but a positive approach means that children need not be labelled and their experience blunted by the expectations this brings.
- Recording is necessary for good practice in early years. Observations, the assessment and future plans should all be written down and a copy, or at least a summary, made available for parents.

THE FOCUS ON INDIVIDUALS

If you focus your attention on one child at a time, with the aim of understanding her current abilities, then you can look in detail at her skills, the confidence she shows and how she behaves. You can build a full picture of her strengths and those areas in which she is less confident or competent, at the moment. Whatever the current abilities of this child you then have a sound basis for thinking ahead to how best to help her to progress. It will be clearer that this child is close to managing a skill or that she could easily be stretched more in the activities that she is offered – perhaps she is in danger of becoming bored because she could manage so much more.

If some of the children in your responsibility are delayed in their development then it is doubly important to look closely at their abilities on a regular basis. You need to check that some progress is being made and in what ways this child needs some focused help. In a busy setting it is far too easy to miss a child who is not progressing in her development but who is 'no trouble' in the group. Some months may pass before it dawns on you that she has the same skill level and narrow interests that she was showing some time ago. If you work in a children's centre or a family centre then some children, perhaps with their parents, will be referred because another professional is concerned about the child's development, behaviour or both. Some centres accept self-referrals from parents who would welcome some help and support.

Children can be affected by stress in the family so that their development slows down perceptibly or they regress in some ways. Good observation and a regular record will help you to pinpoint how and to what extent this is happening to a child. Sometimes a regular record will just be the starting point for your observation and detailed work with a child. Children who are very delayed in their development or whose learning is affected by disabilities will be helped more effectively if you take a more detailed look at particular areas of development.

There are different approaches to assessing and recording children's development but any method should produce a full picture of children at a given, dated period. You should be able to look back and gain an accurate view of how children were managing in all the following areas.

Physical development

Children's physical abilities and their feelings of competence.

- Whether children are managing the larger movements such as walking, jumping or riding a bike and something of how they use their skills.
- A careful assessment of children's confidence in using their skills, since sometimes children are able, for instance, to climb the outdoor frame but lack confidence.
- Fine physical skills such as picking up small objects, pouring or doing up buttons. These skills, even more than the larger movements, involve the coordination of eye and hand.

Communication

This part of a child's assessment includes spoken language but covers considerably more, such as:

- Efforts to communicate, with or without words. A broad look at communicative abilities is especially important with very young children who are not yet speaking.
- Expression through words and phrases as well as understanding of what is said by others.
- The development of communication skills such as listening.
- Language and the development of thinking, for instance, as shown in the understanding of abstract ideas such as relative size or shape.

Bilingual children

Most readers will be working in early years centres where English is the daily spoken language. For many, although not all, bilingual children this will be their second language. It is inappropriate to assess children's second language in the same way as their first. Unless they have learned two languages simultaneously, children will be more fluent in one than the other. Ideally, you need a reliable assessment of a bilingual child's first language but, unless someone in the centre is appropriately bilingual, this may not be a realistic option. What is then most important is that a child's facility with her second language is not assessed as being her total language skills.

Social development

This heading can be broad but could include:

- A child's relationships with adults and other children and friendships formed.
- Life in a nursery or playgroup is different from family life and some observation can be useful of the relative ease with which children manage to make social contact in the group and handle issues such as turn-taking.
- Perhaps this heading might cover children's play – their interests and how they cope with different types of play activities.

The development of self-help skills

- Even very young children may wish to help out in their own physical care, so a note of what they try and can manage is valuable, even with the younger age range.
- Children's abilities to manage with little or no help in feeding, toileting and dressing.
- Observation is also useful to assess whether children feel able to ask for help when they need it. The aim in helping children towards more self-reliance should not be to dissuade them from seeing adults as a useful resource.
- Part of self-reliance is the confidence to offer help to others – either other children or helping out in the centre's routine.

Behaviour patterns

Sometimes an assessment of a child's behaviour is reached through all the other headings, or perhaps included most under 'social development'. A separate section can be helpful especially if a centre is dealing with many children whose behaviour is worrying or hard to handle. It is important, however, that such a section is phrased, and used, as positively as possible. It must never read like a list of complaints about a child.

The exact headings for the different areas of development may vary as may exactly what topics are included under each. For instance, children's ability to concentrate may be included with communication or perhaps in a section on play and learning. What is most important is that a full picture of children results from whatever record form or guide that you use.

DIFFERENT METHODS

The aim of any report

No early years team wants to generate piles of paper so it is important to be clear about your reasons for focusing on the development of individual children. The point of reports on development, whatever the format, is that the information you gather is:

1 Useful at the time. It gives an accurate picture of a child and points towards sensible plans for the future in working well with this individual.
2 A helpful record for workers, and parents, to look back over to gain a sense of a child's progression and changes over time.
3 A pattern of observation and written reports on children's development can also identify strands of work that would be positive for the whole group or for smaller sub-groups of children with similar developmental needs.

Any method of gathering information on children's development is potentially open to misinterpretations and individual workers within a team need a shared understanding of what is being done and why. Your expectations of what you observe can shape what you notice or the sense you make of what you see and hear. Do not overlook how you are part of what is happening, because you are not expected to stand back in the way that a researcher would in observing your setting. You are part of what is happening and may inadvertently influence the situation. You will find practical ideas within this chapter for becoming alert to your own behaviour without becoming detached from the children in a way that would be inappropriate in your kind of setting.

Diary-type reports

It is possible to look at children's progress in an open-ended way, perhaps through keeping a diary record for each child or writing impressionistic reports. The advantage to this method is that a very personal picture can emerge of a child and there can be a real flavour of the most striking events over a period of time. There is a place for diary-type records and some centres find that a daily diary sheet is the best way to keep track of 'don't forget' items about a child's day and communication with parents.

The potential disadvantage, especially if you only use dairy-type records and no other method, emerges from their very flexibility and immediacy. Without a clear and consistent framework, you may be undecided as to what is worth writing down and so each report covers different areas. Without a definite structure to observations and the written report you can easily find that different aspects of a child's play or behaviour have caught your attention each time. For example, a worker's current concern about four-year-old Dudley's expressive language may not be supported by earlier reports because his impressive physical confidence, and application of those skills to escaping from the nursery, dominated previous reports. There is also the risk that problems and worries may take up more space in the report than a child's progress, so again the overall picture is not very accurate.

Reports using headings

An alternative to using completely open-ended reports is to have report sheets with ready-done headings that take you through all the different aspects of a child's current development and behaviour. The worker has flexibility on how the observations are noted down, but is far less likely to overlook entire areas of development. This type of report can work far better than completely open records to provide continuity of information on a child and to offer useful information when someone looks back through previous reports.

An advantage of writing in your own way, but under headings, is that you can possibly describe the flow of how children are learning and give examples of what you have observed. A possible disadvantage of the method arises if workers are loathe to write specific descriptions of what children can manage and a clear picture of the child does not really emerge.

Some settings use a report form with headings to pull together information about an individual child in preparation for reviews or case conferences – see the example in the box.

Example: Part of Dafydd's report

A developmental record with headings needs to be completed with enough information to be accurate but not turn into such a lengthy report that nobody ever reads it. An excerpt follows.

Rhiannon Nursery School report form
Name of child: *Dafydd Roberts*
Date of birth: *3.1.93*
Current age: *3:6*
● **Physical health and emotional well being**
Dafydd has been in the nursery for six months now, although his attendance was interrupted over the winter by two heavy colds and a bout of flu. We, and parents, are concerned that Dafydd's hearing may have been affected by his illnesses. Mother says that he was diagnosed with glue ear a year ago but she did not get to a hospital appointment because of difficulties with her pregnancy (second child). Mrs Roberts says she will contact her doctor to follow this up now.

It was a couple of months before we felt Dafydd had settled (interruptions with his winter illnesses). He now seems happy and has made friendships with Max and Shahana. Mrs Roberts says Dafydd talks a lot about nursery at home and is pleased to come in the morning. He appears comfortable in small groups but is usually not keen to speak up at 'Show and Tell' time or to do anything in front of the whole group. This week was the first time he chose to sing for us (a Welsh song that his grandfather taught him)...

The report continues under the other headings of:

- Language and communication
- Play
- Physical development
- Self-reliance in the nursery
- Behaviour

Completed by: *Olwen*
Date started: *1 July 1996*
Date finished: *5 July 1996*

Developmental guides

Another alternative is to use a developmental guide that has a wide selection of items to cover all the areas of development and a spread of skills and abilities within each. No guide that was manageable for use within a centre will include absolutely everything that children are learning. But anything you use should be detailed enough to give a full picture of children and enable you to identify changes that happen over time.

A helpful developmental guide will have a list of descriptive items for every area of development. The items will usually be listed in approximately the order than children will manage them but individual children vary.

Items are usually ticked if a child can manage them, but it is most useful to have space on the recording sheet to indicate when a child has nearly managed a skill or where there is some doubt about an ability. Some aspects of a child's development cannot be properly noted through ticks, or the absence of a tick. A guide may offer several alternatives to support a description of how a child plays or relates to other children. You would mark the alternative that best describes the child and add your own comments. (See the example on page 28.) There should always be space for descriptive notes about children, for instance how confident they seem in skills and to what extent they use their skills spontaneously in play or need to be encouraged to try.

The first time that you complete a guide on a child can be quite time-consuming, as you work through all the items relevant to her age and abilities. However on subsequent occasions you will find it quicker since you only have to observe for the additional skills that a child has learned and whether her play and general behaviour have changed.

The potential advantage of a developmental guide is that it can provide an accurate 'snapshot' of individual children at a particular time. This will not be a single date since proper completion of a guide can take more like a week than one day. The information can provide a firm basis for future plans with a child, a focus for encouragement and an accurate comparison point to look back on in the future. When a guide is laid out with space for completion on several different occasions the progress, or lack of it, can be clear within the same page (see the examples below).

The potential disadvantage is that workers may focus narrowly on the individual items in the guide or allow their work with individual children to be shaped by the desire that children manage a narrow range of skills ready for the next observation and related assessment. The points that follow stress how important it is that workers understand how to use a developmental guide properly. Some negative consequences of this type of record arise out of misuse and misunderstanding.

Developmental guides are not tests in the sense that they are not pass/fail reports. The kind of guide you would use in your setting would not generate a score for children. A Child Psychologist or Doctor making an assessment of a child might use a different developmental test that would lead to a score. It is important that you see guides as a useful and positive description of children and help parents to look at the information in the same way. Sometimes the guide will highlight that a child is having difficulties or is clearly delayed in development and this needs to be discussed carefully with parents, always in the context of 'what we can do to help'. (Look again at page 19 on talking with parents about their children's reports.)

Example: Morag at 4, 7, 10 and 13 months

Queensmere Nursery Developmental Guide

Large physical movements

Date:	2/4/96	8/7/96	9/10/96	8/1/97
Child's age:	4 mnths	7 months	10 mnths	13 mnths
Can the child. . .? Roll from back to stomach	✔	✔	–	–
Sit without support for short periods		✔ (long time) ✔	–	
Throw objects e.g. rattle		✔	✔	✔

Crawl on all fours	*(trying)*	✔	✔	
Pull self up by furniture		✔	✔	
Stand without support			✔	
Squat down from standing			✔	
Walk with help		✔	✔	
Walk alone			✔	
And so on …				
Completed by	Nasira	Nasira	Alastair	Nasira

Comments on the example:

Nasira, Morag's key worker, has used the developmental guide to note what Morag can manage but has added descriptive comments of her own. When Nasira was away on holiday, her colleague Alastair completed the guide in the same way.

Morag is progressing well for her age but her new-found mobility has raised problems at home. Morag is the first child of parents who take great pride in their home. They are initially shocked at how a mobile one-year-old is 'getting into everything'. Nasira is able to use the pattern shown in the private nursery's development guide to be very positive about Morag's progress and then to discuss, in an understanding way, how her parents might adjust their home to take account of their daughter's mobility and safety.

Example : Jack from 2:6 to 3:0

Social development including play with other children

Date:	5/2/96	15/5/96	20/8/96
Child's age:	2:6	2:9	3:0
How does the child react something that is difficult for her/him?			
Give up quickly			
Try for short while	✔	✔	

Try persistently			✔
How does the child react to a quiet activity that requires concentration?			
Fidgety from the start	✔		
Concentrates for 1–2 minutes at most		✔	✔
Concentrates for 5 minutes or more			
In play with other children, does this child . . .?			
Usually play with other children, join in			
Usually play alone, but near other children			
Usually keep apart from other children	✔	✔	✔

Comments on the example:

Over the period of three observations, Jack has been gaining in his ability to concentrate. However there seems to be little change in his general relationship with the other children. Jack's key worker, Carole, has been alert to how he reacts to children his own age and feels that Jack is nervous of the others. His wariness does not seem to be decreasing and she decides to talk with Jack's parents to gain some perspective on why Jack is reacting in this way, and so towards how she could best help.

Choosing a type of record

Any developmental record needs to provide enough detail – by headings to guide you or items within the different areas of development – so that a full picture emerges of children. However, you do not want the record to become so long that completing them for all the children is a seriously daunting task. This chapter does not include recommendations about what type or actual record to use because every early years setting has to make that decision. Many nurseries and playgroups develop their own record forms by modifying existing forms. There are several books in the suggested reading list on page 56 that would be of help.

Working with disability

If you are working with children with disabilities it is very likely that you will have to modify your pattern of observation to gain an accurate picture. Children with learning disabilities are likely to progress in development at a slower pace, possibly but not certainly in all areas of development. You need to be alert to the finer steps towards managing different skills if you are writing up a report under headings, and appropriate books on children with disabilities will support you as a resource. If your setting uses a developmental guide with items, then it is very likely you will need a different version for children with learning or physical disabilities. The items will have to reflect the fine gradations as the children move towards skills and sometimes you will have to observe, as well as help, children through different channels. For instance, children with a hearing or visual disability will learn about the world and communicate in different ways from children with hearing and vision.

General points about developmental records

There comes a point when some skills are no longer relevant to note down because a baby or child has progressed. For instance, any record of a child's physical development would not include comments about crawling when that child was confidently mobile by walking. If you are using a developmental guide with separate items then you have to use your common sense on where to start, if the guide covers a wide age range from babyhood. A descriptive record that you complete under different headings will naturally move on with the child's current abilities and interests.

Timing
The aim of completing a full description of a child's development is that you have an accurate picture of what he could manage at a given time. This is the 'snapshot' quality, which enables you to compare future observations and gain an idea of how the child is progressing over time, or perhaps not making much perceptible progress. So, for the report to be of most use you do not want to spend a large amount of time completing your record sheet or guide. It is wise to complete your observations of one child over a few days, at most a couple of weeks. The picture can become very confused if the record is part completed, then left, to be picked up some weeks later.

If children are unsettled for some reason or unwell, it is better to leave your observation of their development until the situation is more normal. Sometimes the difficulties you experience are part of how this child behaves in your setting. Perhaps his attention is very easily distracted or she is loath to follow suggestions from adults. If you cannot overcome some of the practical difficulties, then it is best to complete your report as far as possible and add a descriptive note about the child's behaviour – with enough detail to make a judgement later as to whether the child has changed.

In any setting you will need to organise yourselves in a practical way to ensure that you make observations of all the children on a regular basis. You might plan ahead, writing in the diary, so that each week you complete a full report on one or two children. The pattern moves on so that each child's development is checked fully 2–3 times a year.

In any developmental record you have to make some judgements from your knowledge of both the individual child and children in general. For instance, there is no need to take a child through every aspect of different areas of skill each time you make an organised check. For example:

- If the child whose record you are updating this week, showed you last week how he could draw a number of shapes free-hand without copies in front of him, then you can incorporate that into the current developmental report. A diary-type record or notebook can be very useful for this kind of short note.
- If a child a child was dry all last week but this week, when you are completing the record, she had one incident of wet pants, then your notes in that part of the developmental record will need to be that she is nearly toilet -trained, but still has the occasional accident.

Creating the chance to observe
When you are completing any kind of developmental record you will observe some of children's abilities through their spontaneous play – they show you what they can do without your having to ask. You will have an incomplete picture of a child's development if you end your record at that point. How a child chooses to spend her time in your centre is interesting in its own right and deserves observation and some notes (see also page 38). But spontaneous play and self-chosen activities will not give you a complete picture of children's skills and abilities. You then have several choices:

- Demonstrate a skill to a child and invite 'Can you do this?'
  Perhaps you would like to check whether a child can hop on one leg or walk along a chalked line in the yard. Either of these skills require good balance and walking the line requires careful looking. As with many of the physical skills you observe for a developmental record, all you want to know is whether children can manage these skills; you are not checking whether they understand the word 'hop'. So you could organise some physical games in the outdoor area and join in yourself to show what you mean.
- Set up an activity and encourage a child to join in.
  Perhaps you are checking how well a child can manage coordinations such as pouring. Perhaps this child chooses not to join the play at the water tray but does accept your invitation to help you by pouring out the drinks for snack time.

Sometimes you will observe what children do together.

- Invite a child to try out some 'special activities' with you.
  Children usually relish the chance to have the full attention of an adult and can pleasantly surprise you under these circumstances.

You may sometimes be left with doubts about whether a child cannot manage a particular skill or is choosing not to show you. If you have created a welcoming opportunity for the child to try the skill and offered this more than once, then it is probably unwise to press the child further. Make a note of what you observed and express your uncertainty honestly over whether the limit arises from 'Can't do it' or 'Won't do it'.

Be aware of what you are asking
Good observation that leads to useful and accurate developmental records on children requires workers to be alert about their own behaviour. You need to be aware of what

> **For example: Martha**
>
> Brian was able to observe Martha over several afternoons at Boundaries Playgroup and completed most of the playgroup's record sheet. However, Brian realised that he had only a vague idea of Martha's make-believe play. Given her level of language and the breadth of ideas expressed in conversation, he expected that Martha's play would be complex and rich in pretend themes. But it was important not to assume. Brian took the opportunity when re-organising the home corner to ask Martha for her ideas of the next theme. Martha enthusiastically chose to set out a baby clinic for the dolls and teddies. Brian was able later to observe Martha's spontaneous make-believe play with other children during the session.

you are asking and therefore exactly what you are concluding that a child has learned or nearly managed. For instance:

- It is one task to ask a child to copy a circle that you have drawn and left on the table, but a different task to request a child to, 'Please draw me a circle'. The first question encourages a child to show their ability to look closely, to understand a request to copy accurately and to control a pencil. But the second question additionally checks whether the child knows the meaning of the word 'circle' and can hold that image in her mind as well as control the pencil whilst drawing the shape.
- If you show a child a blue car from a pile of different coloured cars and say, 'Can you find me another blue car like this?' you are checking if the child can match for colour. However, if you request, 'Please find me a blue car', with no example in your hand, or ask 'What colour is this?', you are asking the child to identify by colour. Identifying colour is harder than matching a given example (or sorting into piles) .
- Suppose you build a simple bridge out of three wooden bricks. You can invite a child to copy what you have done with 'Now you make your own bridge'. However, the task is harder if you knock down your own bridge, rather than leave it up as a model to copy.

You need to be consistent in what and how you ask an individual child but also consistent between observations of different children. A developmental guide with pre-written items can help towards this consistency, so long as you do not change the wording on items.

Your non-verbal clues
Body language is a natural and important part of full communication with a child. But, when you are checking what a child can manage without help, you have to recall that

your behaviour can shape the observation. For this part of your work with a child you will need consciously to inhibit your gestures. For instance:

- If you are asking a child to pick out a particular object or picture from a selection, then keep your eyes on the child in a friendly way. If you look at the selection, it is very possible that your eyes will be drawn to the object in question.
- If you know that you are given to expressive gestures then, only for the time of your observation check, put your hands in a pocket or clasp them together.

Keep assessment separate from help to learn

Much of your close attention given to children will be devoted to helping them to learn and become confident in their skills. However, you will often have to inhibit this positive desire to help for the period of time that you are observing and checking what children can do without help. For instance, in the earlier example of checking whether a child can pour from a jug into smaller containers you might move to help a child whose hand is wobbling and the liquid is spilling. The help would be a natural thing to do but your notes in the child's record cannot then be that she can pour, but rather that she can with some help.

Making sense of the information

The overall picture of a child from your developmental record needs to be accurate and positive in the sense of supporting your continued work with a child.

A rounded picture of a child

The report should give a balance of what children are able to do or have nearly managed and those skills which are currently outside the children's reach. Comparison of different reports spread over time should provide a sense of children's learning.

A detailed developmental record form or guide should point workers, and parents who become involved, towards any difficulties that a child is experiencing and whether there is any delay in the child's development. Children are not helped by reports that fudge their difficulties but by an honest description, with details that help future plans. (See also Chapter 1 on planning.)

The developmental record form or a guide with lists of items should not be used as the detail for plans in working with child. It is important not to become too concerned about individual items, like threading beads, or just one area of development, such as pretend play, to the exclusion of the rest of what a child can or should be able to do. Certainly plans based on the report should not aim to help children specifically to manage certain items or areas of development by the time of the next observation. So, a sensible aim would not be to train a child to ride a bicycle because that is the next item in a developmental guide. You would look at a range of physical activities that were nearly within this child's grasp and encourage her to learn and practise. If this child seemed, from your observation, to be held back by limited confidence in physical activities then you would not try to boost her confidence just with bike riding but with other activities, especially any that she seemed most comfortable to try.

Development and progress

There are two main ways of making sense of the information that you gather from careful observation and both are equally important.

● **Compare children with their earlier selves**

You can compare children against themselves as individuals with the observations you made at an earlier time. So, you might be considering a whole series of questions. For instance:

1 What can Alric manage now that he was not doing six months ago? We were concerned that he used his language only in very short sentences and had difficulty listening – how is he now?
2 Has Alric overcome his tendency to stay playing long past the point when he needs to go to the toilet – does he still have toileting accidents of this kind? Six months ago Alric seemed to be developing a friendship with Tony and we were hoping that Tony's full expressive language might encourage Alric – what has happened?
3 And so on . . .

In order to work with children as individuals, you need to look for continuities in their own development, to celebrate the positive changes as well as address any concerns in a practical way, based on the information you have gathered.

● **Compare children against developmental norms**

It would not be responsible in work with children to ignore the broader base of knowledge on what children on average will be managing by different ages. Using the yardstick of this child six months ago, she may be gaining in skills each time she is observed. However, the overall picture is very different if she was initially behaving like a much younger child than her years and this gap has widened. Children whose development is delayed in comparison with averages deserve some practical help.

For example: Dorcas

Dorcas is three years old but her physical competence in self-help is more like that of a two-year-old. Dorcas needs to be helped from that position. This type of help does not imply treating her like a two-year-old in all ways but a sensitive shift to helping her in the ways that might have seemed more obvious had she actually been two years old. Dorcas' key worker will need to keep her progress in mind as changes happen and to hold what can be a delicate balancing act between Dorcas' age in years and the stage at which she is operating.

In contrast, children who are progressing particularly well in their development, from the perspective of their age in years, may well need more challenge – not necessarily in all areas of their development – and without that extra stretching may become bored.

There is often concern that referring to material on children's patterns of development may lead workers or parents to label children in an unhelpful way. This is certainly not inevitable and the dangers of ignoring the bigger picture are greater from the child's point of view. It can be difficult to keep yourself fresh on reasonable expectations for babies and children at different ages, but the effort is important for good practice. Otherwise workers can risk becoming swayed by the particular abilities and interests of the current group of children. If you work with a group in which many of the children have developmental delays, perhaps in language, it is only too easy for your mental picture of children as a whole to become that of the group. One risk is that you, and your colleagues, might not recognise just how much you are filling in the gaps in what the children say. A second risk is that the slightly more able children in the group become your yardstick for very able children, when they are average in terms the full picture.

Any comparison needs to be made with caution and useful resources for this purpose give wide age bands. The days of 'at 18 months a child should be able to do these six items' have gone. You could try my book, *Child Development from Birth to Eight – A Practical Focus*, which has guidance on the changes that are reasonable to expect as the months and years pass. (See also the suggested reading on page 56.)

3
∎

MAKING SENSE OF
CHILDREN'S BEHAVIOUR

HOW CHILDREN SPEND THEIR TIME

Spontaneous play

There is often some difference between the full range of what children are capable of and those skills they choose to use when they are given free choice in their play. An organised look at children's abilities (see Chapter 2) can bring pleasant surprises, because some of the children will be capable of more than they usually show you. Encouragement and some specific opportunities allow children to show their potential. Good practice in work with young children means using your skills to extend the choices that children make and to encourage them to explore activities that they might not have taken up alone. Yet, you can still be surprised by the results of observations that form a developmental record.

It is equally worth making time to observe children's spontaneous play and choices. Children are also influenced by the choices that their friends make within your setting and may move towards one activity rather than another, motivated largely by the wish to keep company with friends. This chapter covers some straightforward techniques for observing children's play choices within your setting.

Concerns about children's behaviour

Unease about a child, or a group of children, can be an equally important incentive for observing behaviour. You need a perspective on a concern since a child whom you, and colleagues, experience as hard to handle, can appear to be a problem to the group for most of a day or session. The behaviour that worries you can also overlie any of the more positive sides to a child's behaviour. Careful, planned observations can support you in assessing the seriousness of a difficulty and looking for any patterns that could help a positive approach to the child.

A focus for observation

This chapter takes a realistic approach to observation within your work. Careful observation can be valuable to your practice but this aspect of your day cannot divert your energies wholly away from attention to the children. It is possible to organise some time for a focused observation and you may also be able to learn from observations that students make within your setting.

Within a normal day or session, you might, for instance, decide to observe:

- one child's choices and movement around your setting;
- the pattern of a close group of children who tend to play all together;
- what happens during one particular activity or within a permanently organised corner within your setting.

Realistically, you are probably more likely to assign this time if you or your colleagues are puzzled or concerned, even mildly. Perhaps you sense that the small construction equipment is being dominated by a group of four close friends who are reluctant to let other children into the activity. Or you feel that one child has not settled into the group at all and does not stay long at any activity, but you want a proper check on whether your impressions are accurate.

Awareness of expectations
Your aim in making a series of observations of children's spontaneous play behaviour is to understand better how children use and deal with your early years setting. You may find that some cherished assumptions about what is happening are challenged by your observations, although sometimes your expectations may be accurate and are given more substance through careful observation. When you look over your notes and discuss them with colleagues and parents it is always important to focus on the children, what they may be learning and how. All the practical points made about making notes on page 17 are equally relevant here.

Perhaps you feel that some activities are more valuable than others and this belief may shift your interpretation unless you are alert and careful. For instance, maybe you expect that a child who shows an interest in jigsaws, books and shape-matching games has to be learning more than a child whose favourite activities are physical games in the garden. However, observation of the two children may show that the first child flits from book to book and never completes a jigsaw. Yet, the second child is the prime mover in organising his friends into complex imaginative sequences to which they return over several days and engage in lively conversation about character and plot action.

Reliable samples of time and events

It will never be possible to notice and write down everything that happens, even within a relatively short span of time. You will feel overwhelmed if you try and will most likely end up with sheaves of unintelligible notes. You will inevitably have to be selective, but planned methods of observation can ensure that your results are not unduly biased and are still of use to you.

The most practical way to make a manageable and ultimately useful observation is to select time and/or events in a planned way. However carefully you sample for your observation, caution will still be needed in interpretation of your findings. You are not undertaking hours of research, so your observations could still have a built-in bias. Also you cannot assume that children will behave in the same way in other settings as they have done in observations in your setting. So any conversations with parents about what you have observed have to be tentative and grounded in comments about 'In the nursery . . .' or 'I've noticed here that . . .'

Example:

Take the concern about how a group of four close friends appear to be dominating the small construction equipment. To make sense of what is going on in this group and their rejection of other children for the activity, you would have to make several separate observations over time. For instance, you might discover that the rejection, by words and mild physical intimidation, is mainly instigated by one child in this group. When he is away ill, the remaining three children allow other children to join the table.

Time sampling

If you only make observations at a time convenient to you, given all your other obligations, you may end up with a biased picture because:

- The times of the day that you have observed are not typical of this child or group. You then risk building your picture of a child or children out of only a small part of the whole.
- Other events around these times influence the child or group so you are seeing only one side to their behaviour or interests.
- Times that are convenient to you run the risk of fitting your preconceptions about a child or use of an activity. Even experienced workers can be affected by their assumptions.

Obtaining a representative sample of time and events requires some organisation, or re-organisation, on your part but it is worth the effort for useful information.

There is no single best way to obtain a useful sample of time and events but the following guidelines will help to avoid bias:

- Plan in advance a timing schedule of the observations – when you will watch and note. Different patterns will be suitable for different kinds of observation, as the boxed examples show. Your aim is to select a time schedule that is sensible for what you wish to observe and which gives you pauses between observations in which you can be completing your notes of the period just finished.
- Make sure you have a watch to keep your observations to time. A stopwatch is essential to keep accurate track of short amounts of time.
- Lay out your observation sheets in advance so that you gather the same kinds of

information on each separate observation in a sequence. Leave enough space for your notes. The complexity of your note-taking will depend on the children. If a child is silently watching another activity for half a minute, then your noting task is less stressful than if he is painting a picture, talking to another child and looking around the room within the same time period.

- You and your colleagues may agree a simple shorthand system so that notes do not have to be made in full sentences. In whatever way you agree to simplify the note-taking, remember that everyone's notes must be legible and understandable later.
- Look carefully at your observations when they are complete, discuss them with colleagues, with the child's parent(s) and be open to alternative interpretations of your observational data.

Examples: different patterns in time sampling

One: In Boundaries Playgroup, Bijal is concerned that Miriam has not made friendly contact with any other children. Bijal is aware that she may have missed low-key, developing friendships and so she plans to watch Miriam intensively within the middle hour of each morning session over a period of a week. In each of those set hours Bijal plans to watch Miriam and note down what she does and says for the first minute of each five minute section.

Two: In Kingfisher Family Centre, Gareth has put a great deal of thought into re-organising the book corner to be inviting to children who are not used to browsing through picture and story books. He wants to find out how far the changes have affected children's spontaneous use of the corner.

After discussion with his colleagues, Gareth plans for a period of three days this week to observe the book corner within two hours each morning and afternoon. The schedule is that on every hour and half-hour Gareth will look carefully at the book corner. He will specifically note down how many children are using the corner, their names, whether they are sharing books or looking alone and which books were being used (so long as he can check this without disturbing the children's concentration). Gareth will also make any other notes that strike him about use of the books and the corner.

Event sampling

Sometimes your observation will focus on children's behaviour – again either individuals or small groups. Realistically, early years workers are only likely to make the time to observe behaviour when they are troubled by a child. You will find specific examples from page 44 onwards in this chapter.

Watch how children choose to spend their time.

The trail observation

Another way of focusing on children's, or adults', behaviour is to use the trail observation method. You need to prepare a full-page layout of the room in which you work and mark, in a simple diagrammatic way, the main areas, for instance painting easels, water tray, home corner, internal door to toilets. Choose your focus as in all the other observation examples. There is no way you will be able to track the movements of more than a few individuals at a time. Your choices are basically:

- Do you wish to record the movements of individuals from one area of the room to another?
- Or is your primary interest in recording the comings and goings around one or two specific activities?

Within the focus that you have chosen, select the time span for observation. Because you want an accurate view of all the movements over a period of time, there is little point in observing for periods of less than about 15 minutes at a time and longer periods, up to half an hour, will give you more useful information. Your notes are lines drawn from one part of the room to the other, marked with an arrow to show direction, a name of the child and the time, as accurately as possible.

The trail observation needs some re-organisation within a room because the worker who is observing really has to be freed up to do nothing but observe for the agreed length of time. So colleagues within a room have to discuss the observation and agree to free one person to observe at a time. So long as you have all agreed and understood the focus, it is possible to rotate who is observing in each time period.

Case study: using a trail observation

The agenda for recent team meetings in Mandela Children's Centre has regularly included the concerns of one room team that their children are hard to settle to activities and much noisier and disruptive than the children in other rooms. The centre currently has six sessions of consultancy with Marsha, a Child Psychologist, and an agreement was made that she could observe this room during her next visit, with a view to offering advice on handling the children.

The workers were uneasy about being observed but keen to find a perspective to help them. Marsha undertook a series of trail observations within the room over a period of an hour and a half. On her next visit she sat with the room team to discuss what she had observed and to show them the sheets. The workers' first reaction was to say that the morning of the observation was not typical, the children must have been better behaved and calmer because Marsha was in the room. She did not argue outright but suggested that she was unlikely to have had a calming effort alone. The workers looked at the observation sheets, expressing surprise how some of the most lively children seemed to have made far less changes between activities than usual.

Marsha turned the discussion sensitively to the worker's own behaviour that morning and their judgements as to whether they had behaved as normal. There was some laughter as the three room workers admitted that they had been very aware of Marsha's presence. Further conversation led to the conviction that the workers had definitely moved around less than was their typical pattern. They were sure they had stayed at a given activity and encouraged the children more than usual. There was still more discussion for this room team to follow but the most useful perspective from Marsha's trail observation was the reminder of how adults' own behaviour influences that of the children. The group did seem to include many children who found it hard to settle and were easily distracted. But the workers' tendency to keep getting up and not sit uninterruptedly at a table was a distraction in itself.

Example: observation of Stephen's play

In Rhiannon Nursery School, Olwen has been making observations of Stephen. She decided to observe for half an hour each morning within one week. Olwen's pattern was to watch Stephen for half a minute and then take a half-minute break, completing her notes of what had been happening. The following excerpt covers five minutes in total time.

★★★★★★★★★★★★★★★★★★★★★

Child's name: *Stephen*
Age: *3:6*
Dates of observation: *16–20 September 1996*
Today's date: *17 September*
Notes: *S=Stephen, K=Katharine, D=Damian, T=Tessa (worker)*
10.00 a.m.
S. standing at the water tray. Looking on at 3 other children round the tray. S. tries to get into small space between K. and D. – K. Pushes S. away.
10.01 a.m.
(T. came over from jigsaws to make children give S. some space)
Pouring water from jug. Looks over at what D. is doing. Picks up funnel and uses like D. to pour through funnel and into jug. Smiles to self.
10.02 a.m.
Pouring from arm's length into tray. D. copies S. Both laughing loudly. S. splashes self and squeaks. (Water is splashing onto the floor). T. calls across to stop splashing. S. looks up, listens and brings arm down. D. still pouring from height of her extended arm. S. says, 'She said "Don't". She said to "Stop" '.
10.03 a.m.
K. tries to take funnel from S. but he holds on and says, 'No. No. It's mine.'
K. replies with, 'You're 'sposed to share' and pulls funnel off S. who leaves water tray. S. walks across to T. at the jigsaws.
10.04 a.m.
S. Sitting next to T. looking at jigsaw of farmyard. T. asks, 'What can you see in the picture?'
S: 'Dogs. Some dogs and a man. A man on a . . . riding a. . . .'
T: 'A tractor?'
S: 'Riding a tractor. Lambs, little lambs. They go "baaaa". I saw lambs at the farm, when we went to that farm.'

★★★★★★★★★★★★★★★★★★★★★

In looking over her notes for the week, Olwen asked herself some general questions to fill out her picture of Stephen and his pattern of play:

- On what activities does Stephen spend most time? Does he have favourites? Or activities which he rarely, if ever, joins?
- Does he approach adults readily, or wait until they make a move towards him?
- How does he try to join groups and how does he seem to cope with rejection or unfriendliness?
- Does he talk more readily with children than adults?
- Does Stephen spend a lot of time looking on?

If the rest of the observation was similar to this excerpt then Olwen could be considering whether Stephen needs some help in boosting his confidence in dealing with the more assertive of the other children. Although the focus of the observation was on Stephen, Olwen could also put some thought into whether any children besides Katharine are using the demand to share as a way to get their own way.

Tape and video recorders

Equipment such as tape recorders for samples of children's language or a video recorder can be helpful, but only if you use them within a clear framework of what you wish to observe. Recorded sound or video material is only useful if you assign the time to watch your recordings and consider with care what they tell you.

Children are often especially interested in tape and video recordings and want to hear and see the end result, much as they expect to be shown photos taken in the nursery. Yet observational recordings are not the same as the record of last summer's trip to the seaside and you need to think about the issues. Courtesy and respect towards children implies that you should make the time to let them look and listen, ensuring that no child makes fun of another about the recording. You can find yourself in a more delicate position if the recordings show worrying behaviour from a child or children. Be ready with an explanation that the short recording is just a snippet to help you in your work with the group and in this case there will not be a film show.

Similar care applies to discussions with parents about what you are doing and why. Video tape can be especially powerful and you will need to prepare carefully if you are sharing this kind of observation with a parent and both of you are already concerned about the child's developmental delay or behaviour.

Taped and video recordings of a child or a group should be treated with the same high level of confidentiality that you treat your notes and the child's individual record. The tapes should be kept in a safe place, with other notes, not left around and certainly not used for purposes other than the original reason for the observation. Recordings should not be used as training material, unless you have the explicit and informed consent of the parent(s) and a refusal should be accepted. Tapes should be wiped no later than you would normally destroy the observation notes that they accompanied.

A PERSPECTIVE ON CHILDREN'S BEHAVIOUR

Part 3 of this book looks in detail at a positive approach to handling children's behaviour. This section focuses on observation as one way of gaining a helpful perspective.

First describe the behaviour

There is a difference between labelling a child's behaviour as a problem and describing it. Several adults may agree on a critical label of a particular child such as 'defiant', 'spiteful' or 'aggressive', but this agreed shorthand is not very helpful. Firstly such labels, without careful discussions about how adults will manage behaviour positively, can lead to a negative overall view of a child, seen through his or her 'difficult behaviour'. Secondly, adults may use the same words but have a slightly different, or very different view, on what behaviours from the child are judged to be 'defiant'. If each of these adults observes the child, they may produce rather different pictures because they are looking in different ways. As a result, one adult – worker or parent – might conclude that the child is posing a more serious problem than another adult believes.

Almost inevitably adults communicate in a kind of shorthand when discussing children, especially expressing frustrations. But this shorthand has to be filled out in proper discussion and before any useful observation is likely to result. The boxed example shows part of this process.

Example: Different descriptions of the same child

Sally and Yinka are together responsible for one group of children in the Mandela Children's Centre. Nancy is a four-year-old in their group whom they are discussing in the room meeting, supported by Maggie, who is centre leader. All three adults agree that Nancy is 'uncooperative' but, to help their discussion of how best to deal with her, they agree to take a few moments to write down a short description of exactly what Nancy does that leads each of them to call her 'uncooperative'. These are their written comments:

Sally: Nancy is sullen and uncooperative. She does not join in and takes little notice of what we ask her to do. It looks to me like she is setting out to annoy us, that she likes the drama of everyone flapping about her.

Yinka: Nancy is not at all cooperative in the group. She takes no notice of adults unless you talk to her directly. So you end up having to say everything once to the whole group and then two or three times to Nancy. Even then she sometimes just stands and you have to guide her along.

Maggie: I have noticed that Nancy is an uncooperative child. Particularly at mealtimes when she will not finish her dinner, however hard Sally or Yinka coax her. She just stares and looks sulky. At other times, she just looks through you if you ask her to do something.

The three adults are describing the same child but a slightly different emphasis emerges in each brief description. Maggie has focused more on Nancy's behaviour over meals and on confrontations between the child and adults at those times. Yinka and Sally have focused on Nancy more as a child who is neither part of the group nor acting like the other children. Particularly in Sally's description there is an element of taking Nancy's behaviour as a personal affront.

Adults – workers and parents – usually have to acknowledge that their own feelings are stirred by dealing with children whose behaviour they find difficult. The annoyance that each of the workers feels towards Nancy, in the boxed example, would need to be discussed within the room meeting. Otherwise there is a risk that any observations could be seen as proof that Nancy was a difficult and irritating child, rather than a way to gain some perspective to change her behaviour and take the emotional pressure off the workers.

Consider observations of adults' behaviour

Responsible workers are alert to what they do as well as how the children behave (see Part 3 for considerably more on this topic). Sometimes, it makes sense to undertake simple observations of the adults in a situation. It is unlikely to be possible to release one worker to watch the setting for specific patterns of adults' behaviour, although careful observation can give useful hints – see the example on page 54. However, sometimes there will be a simple observation that will contribute another perspective on the problem.

For instance in the example of Nancy, it would be well worth the time for Sally and Yinka, as workers responsible for the room, to check on how many instructions are being given to Nancy within a day, and to compare this figure directly with their approach to two or three other children in the group.

This type of observation might show that Sally and Yinka, and Maggie when she is in the group, are giving Nancy an unrealistic number of requests. It is not unusual for frustrated adults to increase the number of instructions that they are giving to children whom they do not expect will follow requests. Difficulties spiral and a situation of nagging sets in.

Such findings from the observation would have implications for how Sally and Yinka approach Nancy. Their best strategy might be to reduce the number of instructions, remain calm over meal times and not expect Nancy to respond to whole group instructions at present. Energy would also need to be given to positive times of encouragement with Nancy.

Aspects of behaviour

Once a child's behaviour has been clearly described, not with a shorthand label, then it is possible to plan a useful observation. You are almost certainly going to undertake this kind of observation because of concern about a child.

There are three main aspects of behaviour that can be assessed through straightforward observations in an early years setting:

- **Frequency:** how often does this behaviour happen?
- **Duration:** for how long does the behaviour last on each occasion, or for how much of the day/session does this behaviour seem to be typical for the child?
- **Severity:** can you make a supported judgement whether this is a mild, fairly serious or very serious instance of the behaviour?

You would not observe all of these aspects for every child's behaviour but would make sense of individual cases. For instance, you would not usually ask, 'How often does this occur' about the behaviour of a very quiet and withdrawn child, unless particular circumstances seemed to provoke the child into withdrawing. If withdrawal is a state that seems to be characteristic of the child, then it is more sensible to observe in order to answer the question, 'How much of the day does Ellen seem to spend withdrawn into herself?'

Some examples follow that illustrate how you could develop a slightly different focus appropriately for a child.

Observation for frequency

You can observe a child over a period of days and simply count up the number of times that a specific behaviour or clearly described pattern occurs. This kind of observation is a frequency count. You need to observe for more than one or two days since you want to make plans on enough information to assume that the pattern is representative for this child.

Example: Frequency count

Queensmere Nursery – observation sheet
Child's name: *Jamie*
Age: *3:6*
Date of observations: *4–10 June 1996*
Description of child's behaviour: *Aggressive – Jamie attacks other children, usually smaller than him. His attacks are usually because he wants something that the other child has, but he also lashes out if he is cross. Jamie is not very patient, if other children provoke him, but we are more concerned about the unprovoked aggression.*

Observations of unprovoked attacks – notes made by Alastair and Nasira.

Day	**Total**
Tues. 4th	4

1. *Debbie had the new bike and Jamie wanted it. J. tried to pull the bike away and slapped at D.'s hands. D. would not give in and rode away.*
2. *Jamie cornered Debbie again about 5 minutes later. He tried again for control of the bike and pushed her so hard she fell off the bike. J. rode off on the bike.*
3. *Tried to get through the door at the same time as Matthew. J. kicked out at M. who promptly kicked him back. J. let M. through the door.*
4. *Was told to stop slamming the cupboard door. He rushed off and knocked into Ramona – hard to be sure but it looked deliberate.*

Wed. 5th 1
Jamie seemed under the weather today. One incident – he kicked Andy when they were both in the book corner. Andy did not seem to have started anything.

Thurs. 6th 0
Quiet day! Jamie hit Katie but she had been very provoking, despite warnings from us – poking and tickling J. when he was trying to paint.

Fri. 7th 2
General pushing and shoving in the queue for the outdoor slide.

Couple of minutes later, J. was removed from the queue for pushing. He rushed over to Ramona and pushed her very fiercely, Nasira caught R. in time but a close thing.

Mon. 10th At least 6
We lost count. Jamie was really wound up first thing this morning – biting, pushing, hitting. He became very upset by mid-morning and cried. For a change he let Alastair comfort him. We actually persuaded him to say, 'Sorry' to Andy who was badly scratched in one incident.

★★★★★★★★★★★★★★★★★★★★★

The example of Jamie shows how observation can point to practical issues. Jamie seems to be worse after the weekend and this may mean that Nasira and Alastair will have to be especially vigilant on Mondays, although the situation needs a very close eye all the time. Jamie seems to have very little tolerance of frustration and lashes out at children who are unlikely to defend themselves. The workers will need to look for ways of directing Jamie to handle irritations in a non-aggressive way and perhaps to express frustrations more in words than fisticuffs. Given the pattern, it would be wise for Nasira or Alastair to make time to talk with Jamie's parents in order to explore what may be going on at home and explain how they will have to take positive steps to deal with Jamie's current behaviour in the nursery.

The example of Jamie confirmed the workers' concerns, but sometimes a frequency count leads to a different perspective. Workers may be sure that a child, whom they find very wearing, is being difficult for most of a session. Then, observation by frequency count shows that there are long stretches in each session when the child is not a worry at all. The behaviour that troubles the workers may be especially disruptive in its timing or impact on other children, or touches a raw spot on this worker's view of how children should behave. The previous impression was that the child was a continual problem but what is really continuous is the workers' irritation with the child.

Observation of opposite behaviour
Sometimes it is both possible and helpful to observe for the *exact opposite* of the problem as you describe it.

It is only too possible to become stuck in a negative spiral with a child whom you find difficult to handle:

1 You most notice the behaviour that you find hard or worrying.
2 Your attention is drawn more to dealing with those instances.
3 When the child is behaving more calmly or in a way that you do not find worrying, you heave a sigh of relief and give attention to other children.
4 Consequently, your image of this child remains as a 'problem' and his image of you is of an adult who nags or prevents him doing what he wants.

The sequence is understandable. Any adult who has spent time with children and is honest will admit to having experienced the downward spiral. Responsible workers acknowledge their own part in the spiral and act so as to find a more positive focus. Observation can support this shift towards finding times to be encouraging of a child rather than a imbalance towards 'No!' and 'Stop that!'.

Examples of observation for opposite behaviour

One: In the example of Jamie the next choice in observation for Alastair and Nasira could be to observe for any instances, however fleeting, when Jamie shows some patience with other children, kindness towards the younger or smaller ones or allows himself to be distracted out of a physical response to frustrations in the nursery.

Two: A similar approach could be used in observing Nancy from the example on page 46. Sally and Yinka could side-step the term 'uncooperative' altogether. They could observe and note under what circumstances Nancy follows a request, either without the need for repetition or with only one repeat. Sullen looks or shrugs would be ignored. This type of observation might show that Nancy is more likely to follow a request if addressed by name first or when she is with one adult and no other children. On the other hand, the observation might show that no matter how many times a request is repeated, Nancy usually has to be guided through what is wanted. So an instruction might as well be said once and the worker move straight into a courteous offer of help to the child. Requests to eat up her dinner may never be followed, so workers might as well stop the requests and concentrate on pleasant conversation with Nancy and the other children, thanking Nancy when she has finished as much as she wishes.

Duration or amount of the day

Some patterns of children's behaviour cannot be observed through a frequency count because the question, 'How often?' does not make sense in this case. A child who appears very withdrawn from the activities or seems rarely to mix comfortably with other children needs to be observed through watching at regular intervals throughout the session or day in your setting. In this method you are sampling time rather than events.

Given your other responsibilities you will need to decide on a realistic schedule for observation. You and your colleagues will not learn much if your total observation time is very small because you cannot assume that the child usually behaves in the way you have observed in a very small sample of her session or day with you. A larger sample and observation times spread over several days, ideally a week, give you a firmer basis for generalising from what you have seen.

Two or three workers can divide up the observation time between them, so long as they have discussed fully what they are observing and how they are noting. In the boxed example of Mark, the two workers in the room shared the responsibility of making the regular observations and spread these over four days, taking two mornings and two afternoons.

Example: Observation of Mark at regular intervals

Kingfisher Family Centre – observation sheet
Date of observations: *4–7 November 1996*
Observations made by: *Pippa and Simon*
Child's name: *Mark*   **Age:** *4:1*
Reason for observation: *Mark seems very withdrawn, he sits on his own a great deal. We are also concerned because he rocks to and fro or sucks his thumb for what seems like a lot of the day. Mark does not appear to have made any friends, does not play with the other children and scarcely seems to take notice of them. We feel Mark has not made a relationship with either of us.*

Monday 4 November, morning

10.00   *Mark is sitting in the armchair, rocking to and fro. Does not seem to be looking at anyone in particular.*

10.30   *Out in the garden, looking at children on the climbing frame. Pippa holds out her hand to him but Mark appears to ignore it.*

11.00   *Crying on his own. No obvious reason why Mark is upset. Pippa moves to comfort him and Mark stands stiffly.*

11.30   *Wandering about the garden. He does not seem to be interested in anything.*

Tuesday 5 November, morning

10.00   *Sitting alone in book corner, sucking his thumb. Simon sits down with him, points to picture on open page. Mark is looking at Simon, hard to tell if he is listening.*

10.30   *Crying (quietly) by the door to the room. Simon has just gone to fetch the drinks. Mark did not start crying until Simon left.*

11.00   *Watching another child painting. Janie (Andrea's mother) says, 'Do you want to do one then?'. Mark does not answer but lets Janie set him up at the second easel.*

11.30   *Crying – pushing over accidentally by Daniel. Allows Simon to comfort him, but does not cuddle up like some of the others would.*

Wednesday 6 November, afternoon

1.30   *Standing in the doorway, watching other children in the garden*

2.00   *Sitting in the armchair, rocking to and fro.*

2.30   *Sitting with big rag doll in his lap. Mark is patting the doll but not looking at it.*

> 3.00   Crying, Pippa is trying to comfort him, says, 'What's the matter?' Mark stands
>   stiffly then moves away, goes across to the rag doll.
>
> _Thursday 7 November, afternoon_
> 1.30   Sitting on large wooden truck but not moving it. Looking across at group building
>   with the big bricks.
> 2.00   Watching Simon fix up the paintings. Simon bends down to show Mark how to fix
>   the lower ones in the display. Mark touches Simon's glasses and looks closely at
>   his face.
> 2.30   Sitting on truck again and seems to be trying to move it.
> 3.00   Wandering in the garden, no obvious purpose.

The observation of Mark confirmed the workers' concerns. It is unlikely that the observations, spread over four days, caught Mark each time in an atypical mood. It is a fair assessment to reach, based also on Pippa and Simon's informal watching of Mark, that he is a child who spends a lot of time on his own. He becomes distressed and comforts himself with rocking and thumb sucking, rather than seeking and accepting comfort from one of the adults. Mark seems to be slightly more responsive to Simon and a good plan might be for this worker to draw Mark out of his shell. Mark may be interested in some of the activities that he watches but clearly needs some coaxing to join the other children.

Sometimes this type of observation will show that a child's behaviour that concerns the workers is not a pattern spread throughout the whole session or day. Mark, for instance, might have emerged as a quiet child who did not speak much to adults but who played in an absorbed way on his own and spoke with other children when the situation was not too noisy. The observation would then have suggested a different planned approach from the workers.

How serious is each incident?

Some behaviour patterns are best observed in terms of how long each particular incident lasts, since the behaviour that concerns adults has a beginning and end. Workers still need to discuss the observation before they start, so that they have as similar a view as possible of what the start and finish looks like with this child's behaviour.

The boxed example of Lucy shows an observation of a child that included a frequency count, an estimate of how long each incident (a tantrum) lasted and a judgement of the seriousness of each tantrum expressed through descriptive comments. Lucy was not having a large number of tantrums but the sense of a serious problem seemed to develop because, if Lucy was not distracted swiftly, the tantrum could be lengthy. Although Lucy does have some severe tantrums, the information from the observations

Example: Severity of Lucy's temper tantrums

Rhiannon Nursery School observation form
Observation completed by: *Amy (Other member of staff in the room – Tessa)*
Date of observation: *3–7 February 1997*
Child's name: *Lucy*
Child's age: *4:3*
Reason for observation: *Lucy has temper tantrums. She screams and cries loudly when she cannot get her own way. Lucy is very hard to bring round from a tantrum or to distract from going into one. If she is particularly angry, Lucy will hold her breath for what seems like a very long time.*

Date	Total	Duration
Mon. 3rd	1	About 20 minutes

Very serious. Lucy wanted to go to the library with Tessa but it was not Lucy's turn. She screamed, swore and kicked me. I left her in the corner to cool down. Several times Lucy seemed to have quietened, but when I looked across to see if she was ready to rejoin the group she started shouting again and drumming her feet.

Tues. 4th	2	A few minutes each time

Mild incidents. The two were close together and seemed to be because Lucy could not fit together pieces from the new construction set. I helped her and she calmed quickly.

Wed. 5th	0	–

Lucy almost had a tantrum over who was to look at new library book first. She took a deep breath and held it. I said, 'All right, you get on with it then' and walked away. Lucy followed me almost immediately and we tidied the dressing-up clothes together. She was chatting about her new baby brother.

Thurs. 6th	2	A few minutes, then at least 10

I feel the problem here was that Tessa tried to punish Lucy after I had already sorted out the incident. (Lucy was quarrelling with Shahana and Damian about who was to play with the cooker in the home corner.)

Fri. 7th	1	At least 15 minutes

I came back from taking a telephone call to find Lucy screaming and Tessa shouting. It seems that Tessa had said 'No' to something that I let Lucy do. Tessa and I have to talk!

suggests that she is amenable to being distracted. An additional problem is emerging from adult behaviour in the nursery situation. Amy and Tessa do not seem to be consistent in their treatment of Lucy and they will have to discuss the issues if the situation is to improve. The difficulties with Lucy may not be the only consequence of their not working well together.

OBSERVATION AND GENERAL ALERTNESS

There is no doubt that observations of children's behaviour take time – for discussion among workers and sometimes also with parents – and will probably require at least some re-organisation to allow a useful observation to be completed. The time and effort is worthwhile because useful information can emerge.

Observation of children's play can complement the picture that has emerged from a child's developmental record as well as expanding your impressions of how the children are using the facilities as a whole. Observation of behaviour patterns can help a planned approach to one individual child but can also sharpen up adults' powers of observation in a more general way. The discipline of preparing for and completing an observation can remind you of the need to check your assumptions about children and of how much can be happening within an ordinary day or session.

SUGGESTED FURTHER READING

Bartholomew, Lynne and Bruce, Tina (1993) *Getting to Know You: A Guide to Record-keeping in Early Childhood Education and Care* (Hodder & Stoughton).

Dale, Naomi, (1996) *Working with Families of Children with Special Needs: Partnership and Practice* (Routledge).

Drummond, Mary-Jane, Rouse, Dorothy and Pugh, Gillian (1992) *Making Assessment Work: Values and Principles in Assessing Young Children's Learning* (National Children's Bureau).

Gregory, Eve and Kelly, Clare, 'Bilingualism and assessment', in Blenkin, Geva, A. and Kelly, A.V. (1992) *Assessment in Early Childhood Education* (Paul Chapman).

Henderson, Ann (1994) *Observation and Record-keeping: A Curriculum for Each Child in the Pre-school Group* (Pre-School Learning Alliance).

Hobart, Christine and Frankel, Jill (1994) *A Practical Guide to Child Observation.* (Stanley Thornes).

Jeffree, Dorothy and McConkey, Roy (1991) *Let Me Speak* and (1993), *Let Me Play* (both published by Souvenir).

Lindon, Jennie (1993) *Child Development from Birth to Eight: A Practical Focus* (National Children's Bureau).

Wolfendale, Sheila (1990) *All About Me* (NES Arnold).

PART 2

LANGUAGE
AND LEARNING

4

HOW CHILDREN LEARN

Children learn a great deal by doing, which can include playing, talking, listening and watching. Learning is an active process and it is done by the learner. This is as true of adults as of children. You cannot make a child learn; you can only provide a setting in which it is easy to learn because there is plenty of help and encouragement.

THE INVOLVEMENT OF ADULTS

Why adults matter

Children undoubtedly learn a great deal from each other. Yet children cannot substitute for the close involvement of adults in learning.

- Children do not usually have the patience, or the ability, to repeat something in a different or simpler way for a child who is confused.
- Children are too close in age and level of development to grasp what it is that another child does not understand. This step can be difficult for adults and requires alert observation.

You will notice that some children enjoy helping others, especially perhaps younger ones whom they can show new ways of playing. But this exchange will stop when the children are bored or want to move on, rather than when the child has necessarily learned something.

- Adults are more likely to have the patience to continue, and indeed good practice is that any early years worker develops such an outlook.
- It is the role of adults to persevere when a child is experiencing difficulties, to provide continuity in the learning setting and to strike the delicate balance between encouraging a child to discover and providing guidance.

Adults – early years workers and parents – can make a considerable difference to a child's learning by remaining aware of the approaches they take and their own forms of communication.

Verbal and non-verbal communication

Everyone communicates partly through words and additionally through all the unspoken messages that are expressed in body language. All children are alert to non-verbal communication but, especially for young children, the messages from your facial expression, eye contact, gestures and general body movement are that much more important. Adults look and behave very differently when they say 'No!' as a command meaning 'Stop it, or else!' from when they are pretending to be overwhelmed by a child who is tickling them and saying, 'No. Stop it' in mock fear.

- Children become alert to the unspoken messages from familiar adults and this form of communication can be central to how children learn.
- You encourage a child as much by how you say something as your actual words. Adults who are excited about children's activities and discoveries are helping them to develop a positive outlook on learning.
- Children notice when the words and body language do not match and are likely to react more strongly to the non-verbal cues. For instance, an adult who says, 'What a lovely painting' in a bored, unenthusiastic voice is not giving effective encouragement to a child.
- Children's behaviour is sometimes more understandable when adults become aware of their own non-verbal behaviour. Children are alert to the weakness of words that say, 'Leave that alone' when the tone of voice and tired face says just as loudly, 'I can't be bothered to keep stopping you'.

Young children who are in the early stages of learning language depend on a range of non-verbal cues to help them in everyday settings. A request to 'Please put your tissue in the bin' is usually accompanied by the adult pointing, making other gestures and looking towards the bin. Young children will have also learned what is expected of them, for instance that tissues and other rubbish should go into a bin. So, in order to follow the spoken request, they are drawing on considerably more prior learning than just the words. The non-verbal clues are a natural part of learning but, if you are trying to assess how much a child understands of the words alone, then for that exchange you have to remove all your gestures and inhibit looking in the direction of what you want done (see also page 34).

The importance of encouragement

Most adults have thought at some time, 'Why is it that I get nagged when something goes wrong, but nobody speaks up when things go smoothly?' This imbalance is often carried over into relationships with children. Adults can usually double their positive comments to children without it sounding too much.

Children learn best with plenty of positive feedback:

- Recognition of a child's efforts as well as the end product of their activity, if there is one;
- full use of communication: words but also smiles, friendly gestures and encouraging nods;

- helpful suggestions and guidance when things go wrong, but with friendly support so that children do not feel that mistakes are failures.

The difference between praise and encouragement

The positives in adults' behaviour with children are usually a mixture of praise, rewards and encouragement. These words are often used as if they are interchangeable, but they have different meanings. The differences highlight how adults can best help children to learn.

- Rewards involve some definite event or something tangible given to children: allowing then to do a favourite activity, planning a special outing or giving special treats. Rewards are usually given for the successful completion of an activity or a particularly good piece of work.
- Praise is a spoken reward and tends to focus on the child, with 'Good boy' or 'Clever girl' rather than on what has been done.
- Rewards can be used as incentives when the promise of a reward is offered 'if' the child does something now. Incentives become meaningless if the promise is not fulfilled.

Praise, rewards and incentives have their place, but you have to be cautious with their use. If they are over-used, then children can be resentful that no reward is forthcoming or want to know 'What do we get if we do the tidying up?' But used sparingly, rewards can be effective. Children who are learning new skills may benefit from a reward, for instance a child learning to unscrew a jar may try that little bit harder to reach an attractive toy inside. Children who are struggling to change how they behave may find that extra motivation in working towards a small treat and older children can manage the symbolism of a star chart.

Generally speaking, spoken praise emphasises the child whereas encouragement focuses more on what the child is doing. An encouraging remark would therefore be 'Well done' and praise would be 'Clever boy'. Children tend to be praised after they have completed something, pleased an adult or 'been good'. Encouragement stresses enjoyment, sometimes shared enjoyment in the activity, or the qualities of an action such as helpfulness or patience. Encouragement is used to help a child try out new activities and to persevere when something is difficult. So children might be praised with 'What a lovely drawing', whereas encouragement would be used when efforts were flagging: 'You've done really well so far. I'm sure you can manage this. Let's try it this way.'

There are times for praise, when it is genuine and used sparingly. The risks of praise are that children's view of themselves can vary with how much praise she has received. In this way a child might believe that her self-value goes up and down depending on whether she is praised or not. Today she had four 'Good girls's, but yesterday she did not have any, so was she then not as 'good' as today? Children need to feel confident that their value is unchanging; that they are liked consistently. In contrast, encouragement focuses on particular events and gives constructive feedback on a child's behaviour. For instance, encouragement of 'Thank you for your help; that made a real difference today' is showing appreciation for a particular happening. Whereas saying, 'You're such a helpful little girl' carries the implication that the child may be less valued when she does not feel like being helpful.

Because praise emphasises the successful completion of something, children may come to feel that there is little point in trying unless they can do it properly. So depending on praise as the main form of positive feedback brings the risk that they will not try if they doubt their chances of success. You want children to be able to assess possible success when there is a genuine physical risk involved in an activity, but this is a different type of judgement. Without encouragement to persevere and to enjoy the process of an activity, children may also rush through, believing that adults will only be interested in finished products, in speed or in quantity rather than quality.

It is worthwhile to replace some of the more common words of praise with encouraging remarks and to take up every opportunity to be positive with children.

- Be sparing with remarks like 'Good boy' or 'That's a good girl' and preferably replace them with remarks that communicate more to a child about why you are pleased with them. Depending on the situation, you might say, 'You did well, that's all your dinner gone' or 'Thank you for collecting the plates'.
- 'Well done' is a useful encouraging remark that can said enthusiastically during or after an activity and recognised effort, not necessarily followed by conventional success.
- Relatively empty praise such as 'That's nice' or a repeated remark to many children of 'What a lovely drawing' can be expanded into 'I did enjoy the biscuits you made' or 'I like all the swirls in your painting'.
- Look for a chance to encourage children's efforts and struggles. Of course, the emphasis has to be a positive one: 'That's much better' or 'You're getting the hang of that now, aren't you?'. Insincere or faint encouragement such as, 'I can see you've tried, but . . .' acts negatively as discouragement.
- Any temptation towards the depressing 'but . . .' reservation needs to be turned into a positive recognition of how far a child has managed. You might encourage a child who has not finished an activity with, 'You've chosen some lovely materials for your collage. Let's look at how you could use them.' An offer of help might be best or guidance on where the difficulty lies: 'It looks like you've had some trouble getting them to stick. Show me how you did it. Perhaps there's a better way.'

The unpredictability of punishment

Punishment is a very inefficient way of helping anyone to learn. This applies to spoken punishment through criticism, nagging, ridicule or harping on someone's mistakes.

Good practice in any early years setting should remove any possibility of physical punishment, but you may work with some parents who believe that hitting children is an effective method of making them learn 'good' behaviour (see also page 147).

Children who are punished may still learn but the process is being made far more difficult because the prospect of punishment raises children's level of anxiety and being anxious is not a positive state for learning. Unhappiness about the prospect of being humiliated in front of other children also removes any excitement and enjoyment in learning.

If you think over your own childhood experiences, or times within adult life when you have been learning a new skill, you will realise the importance of encouragement and use of mistakes as a genuine opportunity to learn. Anyone who is nagged about mistakes, or the prospect of making a mistake, can worry so much that they are unwilling to take the risks that are necessary when you are learning something new. The fear of possible failure becomes stronger than any wish to become competent. If the situation becomes really stressful children's, and adults', feelings can be dominated by anxiety and they may appear uncooperative or inattentive to the other person who has actually caused these feelings.

Children can be enjoyably absorbed in learning.

PLAYING AND LEARNING

Children learn a considerable amount through the daily activities of their lives, many of which are enjoyable and absorbing play. The value of learning through play is so much part of early years practice that it can be easy to overlook that not everyone sees the potential link. Some parents may be very doubtful that children are learning identifiable skills and knowledge through nursery or playgroup activities. Several issues can arise here:

- Memories of their own childhood may convince some parents that learning does not happen unless children sit in silence at a table and have some written material in front of them. Unhurried conversations are needed with such parents to explain the breadth of learning that happens within the early years. Displays and open group discussions can also support understanding.
- Sometimes workers have not been clear in their explanations of what they aim for children to learn through the play curriculum. Clearer language, specific examples and discussion about parents' own children can help.
- Do not overlook the reality that, in some settings, parents' doubts may be well-founded. Learning through play is not a magical formula and workers whose behaviour ignores many of the guidelines in this chapter will not support children's learning, regardless of the quality of play materials.

Materials and play equipment

Children need a range of play materials and activities that are sufficiently challenging to stretch them, but not so difficult that the leap from their present abilities is too great. Children will learn both by practising something familiar and by trying something different or slightly difficult. Children who are advanced in their development or more able than the rest of their group may need more challenging activities if they are not to become bored.

Variety in play materials is useful but is not an end itself. There are times when children want to explore or practise more on the equipment that they enjoyed this morning or yesterday. Workers need a plan for what they will make available to the children but the children's views should be taken into account as well. Any setting needs good resources since children benefit from variety in play materials that support similar skills or concepts. Children will cease to learn if the same materials are constantly recycled and frustrated if they link equipment in their mind with not being able to do something.

Children's learning is supported if the materials and activities available are appropriate for their interests as well as their abilities. Children's attention is held by activities that build on and extend their interests. A child who is absorbed by toy cars and lorries may not be enthused by painting or drawing. She may, however, be motivated to use the same materials to mark out a town and system of roads for her cars. A child with a very narrow range of interests should not be left with those limits, but it makes sense to build from the interests that a child has already shown, if they show resistance to trying new activities.

Children with learning disabilities need a variety of play materials that will support learning at the same level of development. They may well pass through different developmental stages at a slower rate than children without disabilities and will become bored with the same play materials. Children with physical disabilities will have special needs depending on the nature of the disability and this will sometimes require specialised play materials.

Learning at home

Nurseries and playgroups are oriented to children to the extent that furniture and fittings such as the bathrooms are scaled down to comfortable child size. The day focuses, or should focus, on children and their needs. When there is a strong emphasis on how much children can learn in the different pre-school settings, there is a risk that parents may feel that their children cannot learn well at home. Early years workers have a responsibility to explain how learning works in their setting but should not imply that parents' responsibility is to re-create the nursery or playgroup at home.

All the points about supporting children's learning in this chapter apply equally to parents but homes are not early years settings and they offer possibilities that are unique. Parents, and other home-based carers such as childminders and nannies, can offer a particularly individual experience to children and can help them ground their skills and knowledge in everyday events. Homes, made safe for young children but still running normally, are also an excellent setting for children to learn self-help skills. Young children often want to help adults and homes offer many opportunities for giving children part of a domestic task and for involving them in cooking, shopping trips and other domestic activities that can only be run in a limited way in an early years setting.

A CHILD'S LEVEL OF UNDERSTANDING

Much of what seems obvious to an adult is new and perhaps confusing to a child. A child has a great deal of information to learn but is also developing a conceptual framework in which to make sense of experiences. New experiences can be exciting to children and adults can share that pleasure. But, as adults, we need to remember how much we know and try to recapture what it was like not to know something. Until you work closely to help children's learning you may never have realised the small steps of discovery through which you passed. To be useful to children, and often to help parents tune in to their children's learning, you need to work hard to see the world as children see it and try to grasp their perspective: to understand what it is that they do not yet understand.

Some adults, even those who have been trained to work with young children, are too quick to assume that children are being uncooperative rather than that they have not understood. You have to unravel to what extent the problem is inattention or lack of understanding, but neither of these difficulties are resolved by assuming that a perplexed child is being deliberately awkward. It takes an effort from adults to work out at what point a child's understanding stops and then to start the help at that stage. It will not help to take the critical approach of 'She's four years old, she ought to know her colours'. If a child is confused, then a genuine effort to help has to start with a child's current level of understanding.

Encouraging children to feel competent

A positive approach to children's learning is more than questions of 'Does she know this?' or 'Can he do that?'. An important role for adults is to encourage children towards a positive approach on learning that includes as much emphasis on feelings as on the intellectual skills and knowledge. You need to encourage children towards:

- interest in and excitement about learning new skills and discovery;
- a sense of competence, of 'can do' that boosts children's self-confidence to tackle new or difficult tasks;
- an outlook that new activities or something that initially appears difficult is a challenge to be tackled rather than a threat to be avoided.

You can encourage children towards a positive disposition to learn by close involvement in their activities as individuals and small groups. You can help by guiding them through plans on how to tackle something new, to follow through and to reflect together on what has been learned. At a simple level you can take this approach even with young children.

Handling mistakes

A vital ingredient of helping children towards a sense of competence will be how you handle children's mistakes. Many adults blithely say, 'We all learn by our mistakes' but do not behave in such a way as to encourage such learning. Children are not helped in the long run if they are left to believe that they have understood when they have not, or that an adult has failed to notice that an activity has gone very wrong for them. But helping a child to face and learn from mistakes will not be achieved if adults show only disappointment and frustration or say bluntly, 'That's wrong' or 'You could do better than that'.

Children can be reassured that mistakes are a step on the way if adults give time and attention. Children make different kinds of mistakes and in different situations you might do any of the following:

- Encourage a child to talk you through her activity so that you can see things through her eyes.
- Ask a child to show you what he did, in the hope that if he takes you through the steps, then you can work out what went wrong.
- Try some simpler questions or a different angle.
- Talk through with a child how a mistake happened, so that she can understand and avoid it next time. Check out what a child thought you wanted. Perhaps she misheard or misunderstood.
- Explain the ground rules of a nursery or playgroup so that the child does not in the future break a rule that she was not aware existed.
- Accept with a child that everyone makes mistakes sometimes and give her the responsibility of putting things right if she can, such as clearing up a spill. Thank her for this.

Children's mistakes can be a source of information for alert adults. Adults often assume that children are illogical, but a far more accurate view is that children often make mistakes that are logical, given their limited information and terms of reference. Their mistakes are sensible possibilities based on what they know so far. (Look also at page 74 on children learning abstract concepts.)

THE DEVELOPMENT OF ATTENTION

In order to learn, children have to attend to what they and others are doing and saying. The ability to attend develops as children grow and with experiences that encourage them. No discussion of how children learn can really be complete without consideration of how they learn to attend.

Learning to attend

Children do not simply learn to attend for longer stretches of time, although that is part of the development. They also learn to attend in a different way as time passes.

Easily distractible
Babies are naturally very distractible; their attention is caught by any new sight and sound. This hunger for new experiences is very useful as babies have so much to learn. Adults can sensibly allow a baby's interest and changes of focus to determine play together, so that the adult goes with the flow. The baby may give a funny face or a bright picture full attention, until something else comes along and the adult shifts with the baby.

Fixed attention
Toddlers have usually moved on from the high distractibility of babyhood and can concentrate on a task or object that engages their interest or curiosity. In fact, very young children can be fixed in their focus. They may ignore suggestions or requests that mean they have to turn aside from their interest. Again, this fixed attention is positive for children's learning from a developmental perspective. Toddlers often explore and examine in great detail. They are not being awkward when they fail to respond since they literally cannot attend to this fascinating sound-making toy and listen to you at the same time.

If you are working with this age group you need to respect their absorption and recognise its value. Make sure you have their attention before you start to speak and be patient. Be ready to distract them from an activity which has to stop and look for any possible compromise. For instance, their detailed exploration of stones on the beach has to end because everyone is packing up to go home. But they can choose one special stone to take away and keep.

More flexibility in attention
Between two and about four years children manage a gradual development of their ability to attend – listening and looking with care. Younger children steadily become more able to tolerate an interruption of their absorption in an activity. They recognise that an adult, or child, wants their attention and stop what they are doing to listen, look or answer a question.

Two and three-year-olds can have difficulty orientating themselves back into an activity from an interruption. Adults who break into a child's concentration should be prepared to help children re-settle if necessary. Remember that children in this age band may still not recognise that an adult is addressing them unless their name is used. A practical step is always to say a child's name before you make your request. If you say, 'It's time to tidy up now, Jon', he may not pay attention until he hears his name because, reasonably, he has not realised that you are speaking to him.

Three and four-year-olds are learning that adults in nurseries or playgroups sometimes address a whole group, but this realisation takes time. Recognise also that an exciting play activity may hold a child's attention so well that she may either not hear you or choose to finish what she is doing before she replies. Take this as a compliment about how well you have organised the activity rather than a slight because you have been ignored by the child.

Double focus attention
Between four and five years old children become able sometimes to attend simultaneously to two demands on their attention. For instance, they may be able to chat and build at the same time, or listen to your suggestion without losing track in her pretend play. When children are coping with a difficult task or a new skill they will have to

revert to a single focus and this is equally true of adults learning something new. With positive experiences of group life, children of this age are also far more able to cope with learning in a group, sharing an adult's attention and understanding that some instructions or explanations are given to the whole group.

Helping children to attend well

Part of helping children is to be alert to their current abilities in attention and to hold realistic expectations. It may be convenient for an adult to expect that two- and three-year-olds should sit quietly during a group story time, but this is an unreasonable expectation of this age group. Patience is required even with older children who have learned to operate in a group but may still sometimes be distracted or fail to register a group instruction.

An important part of helping children in the development of their attention is to behave as you wish them to behave. Listen to what children want to say to you and show that you have listened and taken an interest by the comments or questions that you then make. Look carefully with children and show how you look by making comments and pointing out details with your finger. Take an objective look at the setting in which you are asking children to concentrate:

- Is there space for children to become absorbed in an activity or does one area tip over into another?
- Can children listen with ease in your setting? If there is a continuously high level of noise – adults calling out or radios as background sound – then children may filter out most sounds. They will not necessarily pay attention because one item of noise is addressed to them. There can be boisterous and more noisy playtimes but there should also be quieter times and corners in the setting.
- Avoid shouting in your setting unless there really is a crisis in which you have to get a child's attention fast. Raised voices as a habit can quickly lead to a very noisy setting in which everyone – children and adults – shout rather than speak.
- As far as possible make sure that you are close to a child with whom you wish to speak. Walk over to him if you are at a distance and avoid shouting. You wish to create a setting in which children feel confident they can get your attention easily. This does not mean that children can interrupt at will. Sometimes you may have to show by a smile or gesture that you have noticed a child wants you and get to her the moment you have finished talking with a second child.

Children with difficulties in attending

Some children will need specific help to improve their ability to attend. It will not help to insist 'You've got to listen' nor to use negative labels such as, 'She's lazy'. Some children have not progressed from a pattern of attention that is more usual for younger children and you will have to help them on from that stage.

Very distractible older children

It is a normal pattern for babies to be easily distracted by the most dominant interest in their environment but some older children still show this immature level of attention. This distractibility may show itself in different ways:

- A child may be physically active, moving from one activity to another, rarely seeing anything through to completion;
- the child may stay still but her eyes show you that her attention is wandering around the room, away from the activity in front of her or your words;
- less usually, a child whose experiences so far have been very distressing may be distracted by worries or fantasies within her own head.

It is very difficult to help very distractible children if you always have to work with them in a busy or noisy group. You will need to give them special attention in a quiet corner, a quiet room with few distractions or catch the moment during a day or session. You will not hold the child's attention for long so you need to think in terms of short bursts of focused attention that bring about a gradual improvement over the days and weeks.

It is wise to choose activities or play materials that interest children or else vital energy is spent trying to get children into an activity that does not hold them. If a very active, easily distracted child is only interested in football, then you could play simple games with the ball that encourage the child to plan and look carefully: kicking towards a small goal mouth, rolling the ball towards skittles or bouncing it through a hoop.

Do not try to extend the game beyond a child's ability to attend. For instance, a highly distractible child may post just one brick shape into a posting box. Be pleased with the child and say 'Well done'. After a few times you may be able to say 'Kayleigh, here's another one' as you hand over a second shape. If you persevere and are generous with your encouragement, you will help children to the point where they can manage a sequence of more than one short activity. Only show the child one toy at a time and have the next set of play materials close but hidden (behind your back, in a bag, under the table). Do not bring out the second activity until the first has been put out of sight.

Make sure you have children's attention before you make a request, saying, 'Angela, look at me' or 'Joe, listen now'. Touching a child's hand or shoulder lightly can also bring their attention. You can gently turn a child's head towards an object, or place her hand or fingers onto the toy that you wish her to explore. You may also be able, with some children, to reduce the distractions if you sit them on your lap or sit behind her on the floor holding her gently to reduce the fidgeting.

If a child has trouble in looking carefully then you can play games to encourage close looking and improve eye contact. For instance:

- Games of hiding small toys under a cloth or a choice of larger containers;

- playing peek-a-boo round a corner or up and over a table;
- clapping hands in a game;
- making faces in mirrors.

Many of the games that will help older children learn to look and pay attention are versions of play with babies and very young children. You may well be providing experience that this child has missed.

Older children whose attention is fixed

Some children may not have progressed beyond the fairly rigid form of attention that is usual for toddlers. It is possible that this immature state in older children may not come to your notice at first. Perhaps a child is even thought to have very good concentration because he does not dash around the room. Careful observation, for instance the methods discussed on page 44, will highlight that a child is very limited in his choice of play activities and treats materials in a simple and repetitive way. Perhaps Nasmin always goes to the sand tray and uses the same shape to make sand pies, and she is angry if other children make her break this rigid sequence.

Your first task is to help a child to extend the activity that currently absorbs her, since you are likely to meet resistance if you try to persuade her into a completely different activity. You can sit beside the child and gain her attention by saying her name, holding her hand or gently turning her head – make your decision on the basis of knowing this child. An encouraging smile will help to gain her attention and then you can introduce some slight variety into the child's play – either by suggesting she try something slightly different or by demonstrating it to her.

Patience is required when you are helping a child who is stuck in an inflexible pattern of attention. Be ready to make friendly reminders such as 'Look now' or 'Listen to me' part of your brief suggestions. Children may also be more motivated to break a rigid pattern when the new possibilities have built-in interest and are not too complicated. For instance:

- Shape boards may be a good activity since it is immediately obvious when the right shape is placed. A variation might be a simple jigsaw completed except for the last piece.
- Children may persevere in taking apart a set of nesting barrels in order to find what is making the rattling sound inside (a small object or perhaps some raisins to eat). They may build a tower of bricks if they can knock it down immediately or put shapes onto the type of toy where a lever can be pressed and the shapes hurtle up into the air.
- Show your delight in what a child has managed with 'Well done, Josie!' or 'Hey, Alric, look at what you've done!'

When you help a child who is fixed in her attention, then consider the kind of games that you might play with a toddler. With slight modification for this child's age you will develop a source of ideas.

When children are delayed

If children are delayed in the development of their attention then focused activities need to be planned to help them on from their current abilities. A four-year-old may need some special time with you when you play games that perhaps you would usually play with a two or three-year-old. It is important to stress that you do not have to treat this four-year-old like a younger child in all respects; you are modifying your approach to help his attention. A positive outlook is very important; at no point should the child feel that he is being treated like a 'little one'. You can make the activities simple but still select materials that will not insult him, given his age.

Games to encourage attention

The suggestions that follow for games can be fun in any group of children and a selection may support you when you want to offer specific help to a child who is experiencing difficulties in any of these areas.

Games to help listening

The simplest kind of listening game involves two identical tins or cartons and one has a small toy or bell inside that makes a sound when rattled. Children have to notice and point to the tin that is making the sound. You can vary this game by having different containers and sound-makers and experimenting with different levels of sound.

Another game is to have two sound-making toys, such as a bell, rattle or squeaky toy, and make one silent. Children have to identify the toy that does not make a sound. You can make listening games more challenging by showing children two sound-making toys, removing them behind a screen and shaking just one. Then you bring them back into view and the children have to say which one made the sound.

You might be able to make a tape of ordinary sounds of the street or home and have children listen and guess what is making that sound – perhaps a fire engine, a baby crying, the slam of a door, a telephone or a car engine. The game can be easier for younger children if you have pictures of the different items.

You can also use any everyday events to encourage children to sharpen up their listening skills. Perhaps if everyone is quiet, they can hear the sound of the dinner-trolley in the corridor outside or a bird singing in the garden.

Encouraging children to look

You want all children to look, take notice and interest in what they see. In much the same way as listening, probably the least effective way to help children is to nag them with 'You must look more carefully!' Take opportunities to encourage children to look with care and to comment on what they see.

Your involvement with children's play will give many chances to encourage children to look carefully and often to extend their communication as well. In a simple domestic routine you can encourage children to find items for you, for instance, the car that was put away with the bricks or the spoon in with the forks. Sometimes you can involve children in a simple search, for example 'I put our story book down. I know it's here somewhere close. Now where is it?'. You can be encouraging with a 'Well spotted, Jasmin! I didn't look very well, did I?'.

Indoor activities such as picture lotto or a simple version of pairs can help children to look carefully. Odd-one-out games can also be made very simple. A line of cars ready to start a race may have one facing the wrong way, or in a row of cups one is upside down. You can say 'Something's not right here, is it?' or ask a child 'Can you make them all the same, please'. Children who are practised spotters will enjoy pictures with deliberate mistakes.

Spotting games can be fun when you are out on local trips with a small group. These games might take advantage of surprise sights, for instance the appearance of a robin on a trip to the local park or a fire engine on the street. Otherwise, your knowledge of the locality can help you to set up an opportunity to spot a post box that is round the corner or the flower stall.

Outdoor activities can be just as helpful as indoor ones and will be the best place to start if you are working with children who are not practised in careful looking and prefer outdoor play. There will be items to spot in any outdoor play area and a game of finding hidden items can be played outdoors or indoors. Older children will manage games with simple rules and 'Simon says' or 'What's the time, Mr Wolf?' require watching as well as physical movements.

Any of these activities can be fun for children whose attention by looking is progressing well for their age. If you are especially concerned about a child, then make sure that the chosen activity is simple. Children will not learn to look if the rules of a game are too complex.

Helping children to remember
In order to learn children also need to remember. Children who have difficulties in attention often also have problems in remembering, but it can take careful observation to work out what is happening. Perhaps children forget quickly, but they may find it hard to give the concentration necessary for recall or perhaps they were not listening well in the first place. There is no point in getting cross with children who are forgetful but you can help them if you are patient.

You can involve children in tasks within the normal routine that give them practise in remembering. Ask children to fetch you items from across the room; they have to recall not only where these are usually stored but what you asked them to fetch. You might also ask a child to take a very simple message to a colleague across the room. Conversations along the lines of 'Do you remember when . . .?' can encourage children to recall the recent past, perhaps only that morning. Your interest through conversation also shows that you value your time with the child.

Memory games can be made very simple. Since attention problems may be linked with children's difficulty in remembering, make sure that you have a child's attention before you give an instruction. Once children can distinguish sounds, you can introduce a game of copying a short sequence with different objects that they can hear. You might show a sequence of shaking a bell and then hitting a drum. A child then copies this with her own set of instruments. The sequence can get slightly longer and perhaps develop into very simple tunes. Another game is for a child to remember a short sequence of small toys posted into a cardboard tube. You post a sequence of car – brick – little ball and the child has to do the same with her tube. She is being asked to remember for a very short time but if this is still difficult then start the game with you and the child posting at the same time and then hold the child back a couple of seconds with, 'Stefan, watch me. Now you do it' for each item in turn.

You can develop all kinds of games that ask children to hold a memory for a short period of time: hiding two objects then finding by the child, requests to 'Touch your toes, then your head' or simple hop, skip and jump sequences. Memory games can become more complex and children often enjoy the challenge. Try simple versions of the party game of remembering objects on a tray that are then covered with a cloth or the round game of 'I went to the zoo (or the shops) and I saw (or bought) . . .' Once children can manage this kind of game you have moved them on to sharpening up their skills of remembering rather than dealing with a difficulty in skills.

LEARNING ABSTRACT IDEAS

Recognise what children are learning

From about three years onwards children are learning many abstract ideas that are used to describe the world. Adults are very familiar with these ideas and unfortunately that can lead them to believe that the meaning of ideas such as shape or colour is obvious. In fact children's learning task is complex and it would be surprising if they did not become confused sometimes. You will be of far greater help to children if you look at their world through their eyes and appreciate the task that they face.

Sometimes adults unwittingly make children's task harder by being slapdash in how they use words. For instance, the word 'bigger' is used to mean taller, fatter, heavier and even older, as in 'When you're a big boy, you'll go to school'. Children's learning survives a great deal of adult laziness in speech but they will unravel the different ideas more quickly if you use 'tall', 'short', 'heavy', 'older' and so on in a consistent and accurate way.

Children need plenty of practical experiences to link the abstract idea or concept with what they see, hear and feel. They have learned a great deal about naming and doing words but 'red' or 'fast' are neither objects, nor actions you do. The words offer a way of describing or contrasting between objects or actions.

It is a sobering experience to list all the abstract ideas that many four-year-olds will have grasped, completely or in part. Try doing this as an exercise and you will easily fill a sheet of paper and more. For instance, they are learning about number, shape, size and colour but also temperature, texture, speed, and the complexity of family relationships, of birth, illness and of death.

Children are not only grasping a lot of new information, they are also learning new frameworks into which to fit new ideas. Theories are tried and abandoned or developed in different directions, especially with adult involvement and help. Children can be perplexed because different frameworks are equally possible in theory. Their struggles to understand can give rise to endearing anecdotes but these stories are also invaluable insights into children's worlds. A personal example came to me when my son was four years old. He asked me one morning, 'Are my T-shirts getting small?' Puzzled, I answered, 'No' and before I could ask any more Drew said 'Well am I getting bigger then? Because Tanith's got my red T-shirt now.' He was searching for an explanation of why his T-shirts now fitted his younger sister but not him. A world in which clothes got smaller would explain this oddity just as well as one in which children get larger. You will find other thought-provoking examples in Donaldson (1980) and Tizard and Hughes (1984) – full references on page 112 – but collect some of your own anecdotes.

Words can confuse

When children are still learning spoken language, adults are more inclined to turn to gesture and showing what they mean when the words clearly will not work alone. However, when children have a good working command of language it is possible for adults to forget the value of showing and creating an activity in which children can experience what is meant. If words have not explained an idea well, then further words alone will probably only add to the confusion. Children who are learning abstract concepts may become very confused and unhappy if their peers do not seem to share their difficulty. You will help by finding activities that focus on visual recognition and on simple like-unlike activities.

Many of the abstract concepts that children learn require subtle visual discriminations. Learning about colour, for instance, requires children to ignore many other features of the different objects that they are told are 'blue'. Perhaps they have learned so far that this collection of objects include a jumper, a brick, a toy car and a bike. Now an adult is saying that they are all 'blue'. But additionally, the jumper feels 'soft', the brick feels 'hard', the car will go 'fast' if you push it and the bike has 'round' wheels. Children distinguish all these different ideas with a variety of experience and patient adult help. They do not learn one area of abstract ideas all in one go but steadily, a bit at a time. The following examples are of learning about colour and number – not because these are necessarily the most important ideas but they do tend to be to the fore with many early years workers. The points made are just as applicable to other ideas.

Learning about colours
Looking at how children learn to distinguish and name colours can highlight the valuable adult approach of thinking 'What do the children need to understand before they will have grasped this idea?'

In order to understand the whole idea of colour (or shape and size) children have to recognise visually what you are talking about. They have to be able reliably to distinguish between red and blue (or round and square) before they will learn the right word to describe the difference they can see. So the games you play to help children have to move from matching or sorting games onto games in which children have to identify objects. In terms of colour, a child first learns to match different colours by paying attention to what she sees and then judging whether a brick or a car is the same, or different, from another one. In a matching game, or one of sorting objects by colour, children have a model for comparison. This is a simpler task than requiring a child to produce the correct answer to 'What colour is this jumper?' or 'Find me a blue plate'. These two questions ask them to identify by colour.

When children grasp colours without too much confusion, you may not notice the move from matching to identification. A child who is confused may appear to be answering at random and needs to be given activities at the simpler stage.

The simplest level of colour matching is to have two containers, such as plastic cereal bowls, in two primary colours, perhaps red and blue, and a collection of smaller objects which are identical (all cars, all bricks) expect that some are red and some blue. You show the game to a child by picking up one brick, looking carefully, lining it up against the same colour bowl and putting it in. Perhaps you will almost put a blue brick into the red bowl and then say 'No' or shake your head and put it into the blue one. Offer the child a chance to have her go. Your conversation during the activity is about 'same' and 'different', not colour names. Under-twos can enjoy this game and often like sorting through piles of objects. The approach can help you build the understanding for a four-year-old who has become very confused. You take her back to the stage of seeing the difference and leave the colour words aside until she is ready.

Sorting and matching activities can be extended, slowly if the child is confused, to bring in other primary colours and sorting out play materials without the bowls to provide a comparison point. A collection of bricks might be used to build different colour towers or paper cut-outs might be sorted into the green and the blue families.

Colour names can be introduced naturally into the conversation but as information for children, not as the pressure of 'Tell me what colour this is'. You might say 'I'm building a red house, can you find me another red brick like this one?', 'Do you want some more green paint?' or 'Is it the yellow blanket you're looking for?'

Learning about number
Children gradually build their understanding of number. Some adults place too much emphasis on 'She can count up to twenty'. Without understanding, such counting is more like a nursery rhyme learned but not grasped. However, counting in sequence is important, since one aspect of number that children need to understand is that there is an order: two follows one and ten comes long after three. Or as one nursery school child delightfully informed me as we talked about birthdays, 'Did you know? You have to be three before you're allowed to be four.'

Children need also to practise their counting skills by counting objects and realising that you stop counting when you have run out of plates or shells in the picture. Once they have experienced getting or counting a certain number of objects, children can make sense of a request to 'Please give me three bricks'. Children may also like counting as a way of measuring their environment: how many stairs or how many steps along one side of the play area?

Numbers are also a way of becoming more definite about general ideas of 'more', 'less', 'not many' and 'a lot'. Games that help children to work with sets of objects enable them to make a visual check of number. Involvement in simple domestic activities often also gives opportunities. You may play with putting hats on dolls, laying out a pretend tea party, building brick towers or planting bulbs in pots. All these activities give scope for exchanges such as, 'Let's count the pots ... Right that's five. So you count out the bulbs for me. We need one for each pot, so that's ...?' When there is an item missing you have scope for comments such as, 'We need one more hat' or 'We're missing two spoons for our tea party'. Children may count with you how many people there are for tea today, so how many plates do you need to lay the table?

Through games and songs children also start to understand the basics of adding and subtracting: the rhyme 'Five currant buns in the baker's shop' or a game of 'I've got six cars in my car park' when children count the cars and then you take one away, 'Now how many have I got?' Although your job is make learning enjoyable and straightforward through the play, always remember and appreciate the complexity of what the children are learning.

LEARNING AS A POSITIVE EXPERIENCE

Babies and very young children are poised and ready to learn. They have a consuming interest in the world around them and are keen to explore, within the expanding boundaries set by their physical abilities. Children can find enjoyment and great satisfaction as they continue to learn within early year settings and the quality of adult involvement will make a difference to the nature of their experience of learning.

Supporting children's learning within a group requires some additional attention to how you relate to individuals, share out your time and attention and keep track of what is happening through observation. In a group, children gain additional opportunities for learning through the companionship and support of other children. However, you also have to be aware that individual links in learning can be lost for children without your input and that children need adults for effective learning as well as other children. Young children, especially the under threes, can get lost in a group, either because activities are dominated by older children in a mixed age grouping or because younger children need the focused, individual attention that can be forgotten if a worker's outlook is too dominated by thinking of the group as a whole.

5

USING LANGUAGE TO SUPPORT LEARNING

POSITIVE USE OF ADULT LANGUAGE

Children will learn from many different kinds of activities: play with other children and with an adult, through quiet thinking or watching and through conversations in which they are allowed to determine the direction and topic as often as adults.

In an early years setting your time and attention is spread between many children and it can be tempting to direct most of your exchanges with children in order to make what seems like the most of the time. However, children will not learn as effectively if they are rarely given the space to determine some of the conversation and an over-emphasis on question and answer exchanges by adults will probably not show children's abilities in the most accurate light. It matters what adults say and how they express themselves but effective adult communication for children's learning is as much being on the receiving end of their attempts to communicate as talking with them in your turn.

Communication with very young children

The building blocks to good communication start with interaction in the very early months. Research with young babies has established how much they seek contact, watch carefully the faces of familiar adults and communicate themselves with sounds, facial expression and gestures. Several features emerge as important in the experience of babies whose ability to communicate develops well:

- There are affectionate two-way exchanges between the baby and parent or other familiar carer. The exchanges are of smiles, friendly facial expressions and sounds.
- The best communication style from the adult is slightly higher pitched than normal speech, with plenty of expression and pauses for the baby to reply.
- Adults respond to attempts from the baby to engage their attention, with shouts, smiles or gestures.
- It is important that the adult and baby take turns. Video recordings of young babies have shown how they make sounds, smile or wave arms and legs in expressive gestures and then pause and look expectant. The basis is being laid for the turn-taking of conversation.

From about nine months onwards there are clear signs that babies are using existing skills to take part in, to continue and to initiate communication with adults and friendly older children. Babies use a combination of gestures and sounds to attract the attention of others and to direct it towards what the baby wants to request, complain about or share as something of interest. As toddlers learn recognisable words, these are also brought in to achieve a number of aims for communication. For instance:

- to name objects or people, with a clear pleasure in being able to do so;
- very simple descriptions, using few words and plenty of gestures;
- acknowledging that somebody has arrived or is leaving;
- communication about events – that something has happened, which may be interesting, surprising, worrying or require some action from the adult;
- to question what is happening or the whereabouts of a familiar person or plaything;
- to implement a strategy to try to get out of doing something.

If you work with very young children it is important to think in terms of your whole communication with them, which inevitably involves giving them undivided attention for periods of time. Young children cannot learn to communicate well if their experience is almost always within a group, with limited direct personal communication. Good practice in any early years setting with very young children has to involve an adult-child ratio that allows workers to focus on individual young children in turn.

You need to be alert and respond to the nuances of what children are communicating. As young children learn to speak, their few words will be supported by tone of voice, gestures and facial expression. One or two words can carry several different meanings depending on children's way of expressing themselves. So 'cat' said with a questioning tone and a look around might mean 'Where's our cat gone?'. Said with satisfaction and an excited pointing, the single word might communicate clearly 'There's our cat!' Expressed with uncertainty and a puzzled look at a picture of a tiger, the word might mean 'Is that a cat? It looks like one but is it really?' Said with great sadness and looking at the body of a strange cat in the gutter, the meaning could be 'Poor cat. Can we make it better?' An alert adult – parent or other carer – would reply appropriately to the child's whole communication in each instance.

There is a delicate balance between hearing and seeing the communication that is not in actual words and filling in too much by guesswork. But a young child who is confident of an adult's interest in her communication will often persevere when that adult has misunderstood or tolerate the mistake on this occasion.

Listening to children

Programmes which focus on what adults say to children can lack an emphasis on adults' listening, and on allowing children to direct the exchange sometimes in the direction that interests them. Good practice in early years work will be to pay attention to what children would like to say to you. Four- and five-year-olds can sense when an adult is not really listening. Sometimes the clues are very obvious, for instance the adult turns away while the child is still talking. But children also sense the limits of communication with adults who most often ask questions for which they have the answer and only take from what a child has said to move in a pre-determined direction. Some exchanges will be of this nature, especially in a group of children, but much will be lost if this is the main form of communication.

Be alert to your own communication since, if you are over-eager in taking the lead in exchanges with children, the likely consequence is that they will not learn so well and that you may inadvertently cause children to be passive in communication with you. A further consequence is likely then to be that you underestimate children's abilities since they do not persevere in exploratory conversations with adults who insist on controlling the communication.

Talking with children

The speech of adults is a major influence on children's language development. Familiar adults with whom children spend time show them, whether intentionally or not, the possible patterns of communication:

- The vocabulary used and the extent to which adults are prepared to adjust their speech to enable children to understand;
- the different uses of language in exchanges (more on this on page 82);
- patterns of behaviour in communication including respect through listening to others, the extent of interruptions and the level of interest shown in what others say. Children imitate these behaviours as much as they learn in other ways from adults;
- learning more than one language – a normal state of affairs in some families.

It will make a difference when adults take the trouble to talk *with* children rather than *at* them. This shared nature of good communication is just as relevant when children do not yet talk as for when the recognisable words come. Children need to be given the space to reply: partly for the actual pause in conversation and also the expectant look on your face that says you are waiting and interested in what the child has to contribute. Your talk with children, whether a brief or longer exchange, will be most useful when it takes account of an individual child's language ability, her understanding and speech. Of course, children will not always understand what you have said but this will not be a problem if you are prepared to explain, re-phrase your comment or to pick up clues from the child that will hint where her understanding or expressive ability has halted the communication (more on page 90).

Adults make a difference to children's language development by making conversation an enjoyable experience. There will be unavoidable times when your comment has to be of the 'Please don't do that' variety but these times must be outnumbered by enjoyable and shared exchanges. Your awareness of your own communication will allow you best to help children. One positive approach is to become more alert to the different uses of speech in everyday communication with children. The next section covers this topic.

USES OF SPEECH

Full communication is not measured by the total number of words or how long someone continues to speak. The value of communication can be seen more in a variety of uses of language. There are two reasons for you to consider use of speech:

1 You will help children if you are alert to the breath of your own communication and how you could open up further possibilities.
2 Children can learn, with your help, to use their own language abilities in different ways.

Asking questions and giving information

Answering children's questions
Adults can be valuable providers of information to children. You need patience because one question may follow another. Answer as clearly as you can and be willing to adjust what you say so that a child can understand, or when you realise that the child was asking a different kind of question to that which you first thought.

The conversation in the boxed example is exactly the kind of exchange that can be hard to sustain in a group situation, such as a nursery or playgroup, because other children often intervene. You may find that your exchanges with individual children remain quite short when you are all involved in an activity such as a craft or other table-top activity. However, look for the opportunities that can arise when children help you within the group routine or come and sit beside you on a bench in the garden. These can be the times for a more relaxed, less interrupted conversation.

For example:

JO (CHILD – 4 YEARS):   Where's Mummy? I want her now.
CHRISTINE (NANNY):   Mummy's working at her office.
JO: But when is she coming home?
CHRISTINE: She'll be here after we've had tea.
JO: But when do we have tea?
CHRISTINE: We usually have tea at 6-00.
JO: What's 6-00? Is it soon?
CHRISTINE: Well, it's 3-00 now. First we are going to pick Anya up from school.

> Then we'll all come home and watch your programmes. Then I'll make tea and you can help me. Then we'll eat tea. And we usually hear Mummy's key in the door when we're clearing up, don't we?
>
> JO: Chris?
>
> CHRISTINE: Yes?
>
> JO: When do you work in your office?
>
> CHRISTINE: I don't have an office, Jo. My work is here with you. Some people work in an office, like your Mummy does. And some people have different kinds of work. My job is looking after you and Anya while your Mummy is away.
>
> JO: Me and Anya – we're your office.
>
> CHRISTINE: Yes (laughs). In a way, you're my office.
>
> And so on . . .

Once children understand the formula of questioning, they may ask many questions and a patient adult that follows a child's own route can support their learning. You have to listen carefully and recognise what, exactly, a child is asking. Sometimes, as hard as you try to look through a child's eyes, you may not fully answer their questions. But children will recognise your efforts and come back later with further questions when they wish. Children who are brushed off by adults will cease to bother to ask.

Young children sometimes use the question format indiscriminately to open up a conversation or to keep one going. Perhaps you experience a sequence of 'Why . . . why . . . why?' when you have given a simple reply each time. Rather than losing patience with a child it is better to call a halt with a comment like, 'I'm sorry. I can't think of another way to explain it. Let's try something else.' Some children learn a formula such as, 'Do you know what . . .?' to get your attention and then there is silence because they do not have anything else to say. Again, they deserve patience from adults rather than irritation. Give children your time and attention for what they are doing or draw them into an activity and talk with them.

When you ask the questions

Often you may ask children simple questions like 'Have you seen the pencil box?' or 'Would you like another sandwich?' These questions ask for a 'Yes' or 'No' in reply, although the first question implies that more information would be welcome if the answer is 'Yes'. These are closed questions and they are useful when you want a simple reply or are checking what a child knows, for instance the name of an object or 'how many?' objects are on the table.

Open questions invite more than a one-word reply. Try to ask a mixture of open and closed questions and especially use open ones when you are encouraging children to explore, explain or tell you more. For instance:

- You may sometimes ask a child of his painting or building 'What is it?'. But also ask open questions such as 'How did you make that?' or 'What did you do to get those lovely swirly bits?' Children are then encouraged to tell you more and perhaps to show you their technique.
- If children volunteer what they did at the weekend, a closed question would be 'Did you like the park?' or 'Was it fun at the pool?' An open question would be 'What did you see in the park?' or 'What did you do at the pool?'

Questions can be useful to help children to explore particular play activities and to pursue their learning of concepts, but can be over-used. The key issues that emerge from sometimes rather contradictory research are:

- Adults' taking an active role through adopting a focused, questioning style has made an impact in some special programmes focused on helping children's learning in specific areas of understanding.
- There is no evidence that making this questioning style the major part of adults' daily interaction with children will help them learn faster. Such a style may actually get in the way, since children find ways to avoid and not reply to adults who are relentless questioners.
- More intensive question-and-answer sessions are better kept for focused work with individual children. A positive learning environment is one in which children feel confident to ask questions and express opinions rather than being mainly required to answer questions put by the adult.

When children are given opportunities to express themselves, they explore their own thoughts and ideas. Adults will also gain an insight into how the children think.

Telling and describing

Telling a child about something is more than just giving information; there is a more detailed, descriptive quality. You may be telling a child a fictional tale or recounting an incident for the child's interest. Children are often interested in the lives of familiar adults, either to hear about the exploits of these adults when they were children or to hear what may seem to you like mundane details of your life. When you work with children it is fair and appropriate that you have a personal life separate from work, but you can share some details of your life away from playgroup or nursery. Children are often interested to hear you describe how you had an interesting visit at the weekend or to hear about your own children if you have them, or what your pets have been doing.

An alert adult listener can encourage children's attempts to describe past and present events and to imagine or plan for the future. The abilities of younger children to describe tend to focus on the present but your attention and encouragement will help them as their time perspective extends. You might prompt children to describe what they are doing at the moment, for instance talking about the illustration in the book that you are enjoying together. Alternatively, the description might be about the recent past: yesterday evening or the weekend, activities or enjoyable television programmes.

Shared past experiences can also be a rich source of conversation between adults and children, started by 'Do you remember when we . . .?' Some of your reminiscences may be special trips which children often like to relive through the re-telling. You may also extend the value of trips by craft activities or making scrap books but never overlook the sheer pleasure that many children experience in simply talking about an enjoyable outing. Even local trips that may seem run-of-the-mill to you can have generated interesting events for children.

You can also encourage descriptive use of language in the simple situation where a child asks, 'What are you doing?' Sometimes you will judge it appropriate to explain but other times you might put the question back with, 'Have a look. What do you think I'm doing?' Perhaps you are involved in a sequence such as mending some play equipment or changing a younger child. You might follow on the child's reply with 'What do you think I'll have to do next?'

Speculation and imagination

You can encourage children to go beyond the immediate by prompting them to wonder and speculate.

- Some simple science or cooking activities are appropriate times for speculations such as 'I wonder what will happen when we add . . .?' or 'What do you think would happen if I put in another ice cube?'
- Talking about books can lead naturally to wondering about 'What do you think will happen next?' or 'What is she thinking, I wonder?'
- Games with cars or hand puppets can also be a positive setting for imaginative uses of language.
- Play in the home corner, pretend tea parties and doll play can all be useful settings for rich use of language between children or with your involvement.
- Children enjoy making up stories which involve an imaginative use of language. A small group of four- or five-year-olds may manage a simple story line that is developed by one child after another.

You can encourage children to use their words as a channel for imagination so long as you relax and let your imagination flow.

Making suggestions

Both adults and children can use language to offer suggestions to others. You might make different types of suggestions to children.

- Suggestions can direct a child in order to help: 'Perhaps if you tried it that way round'.
- Questions might also be implied suggestions: 'Would you like to try a more difficult puzzle? This one's very easy for you.'
- Statements might also include a suggestion: 'I think the baby would like a rattle. Why don't you chose one?'
- Questions can directly invite suggestions and opinions from children: 'Where do you think would be the best place for this poster?' or 'What do you think the man should do with that naughty dog?'

Making genuine suggestions when talking with children can create an atmosphere in which there is more equality between adults and children. You may have to determine many of the details of children's lives but there is still scope for them to make decisions when you give them the space. Suggestions which are said more like instructions will not have the effect of inviting children in the same way. Children who have been encouraged by adults are far more likely to offer their own ideas without prompting, with 'Why don't we . . .?' or 'Can we do my idea?'

Children look to adults as a useful resource.

Explanations

Some replies are explanatory as well as or rather than giving information. A good explanation can help a child to understand more or to look carefully: 'That bus isn't working. Can you see it's got a flat tyre.' Sometimes an apparently simple request to a child needs a follow-up explanation: 'Can you get me the dustpan and brush, please?' followed by 'It's under the chair in the corner.'

Short explanations given in irritation are not usually helpful; 'Because I say so!' does not add much to a child's understanding. Longer explanations might offer a justification that children can accept even if they disagree: 'No, I told you. No television until we have put all your toys in the box.' In a question-and-answer exchange with a child you may have to work hard sometimes to phrase an explanation that a child can follow.

Young children can find it hard to explain without guiding questions from adults which help them to focus attention on relevant parts of what they can see. A question such as 'What do you think has made the puddles dry up?' requires children to have a source of general knowledge. Some may have an idea about the heat of the sun but others may try an answer about water 'just going away'. Such an exchange needs to move on from what the child currently understands and to add some information. Children can enjoy a relaxed atmosphere in which they are asked to explain because it boosts their confidence; adults are showing that they believe the child has information and understanding.

Some requests for explanations from children do not usually lead to useful replies; these are the demands for a justification of 'Why' a child has behaved in a certain way. Questions about wrong-doing such as 'Why did you hit Sara?' or 'Why did you wet your pants?' are heard accurately by children as criticisms and usually result in silence or muttered comments like 'Because' or 'I just did'. You may get something more useful from a request to 'Tell me what happened with Sara and you' or 'You waited too long to go to the toilet, didn't you? What happened?'

Requests and instructions

Some use of language is to direct others. Often you will be guiding a child through requests like 'Please bring me another fork' or instructions like 'You can be fierce when you knead pizza dough. Watch me.' It can be an enjoyable and refreshing experience for children to have an adult as assistant rather than vice versa. For this to work, you have to be prepared to attend and follow instructions and perhaps to pretend a little that you are unclear about something. Children can then gain the experience of using their language to direct you. It is preferable that they practise on you rather than only on other children, since you will be in a better position to avoid being irritated by what may be rather peremptory remarks of 'No, not like that! Like this!' An adult is also able to guide a child towards giving clearer instructions, for instance 'So, I'll build this bit of the station shall I? Do you want me to use just blue bricks like you? Or can I use whatever colour I like?'

A balance of encouragement over criticism

Spoken words, as well as all the non-verbal messages, can be used to communicate positive or negative opinions and judgements. Adults sometimes spend proportionately more time making critical remarks than in encouraging what has gone well (see also page 60). Watch out for using all the opportunities to say 'Well done' or 'Look at all your hard work'. The type of remark that says bluntly 'You're silly' or 'That's the wrong way to do it' is not helpful to a child. It gives no guidance on what to do better next time and, even worse, has the effect of chipping away at a child's confidence to try another time. To avoid a discouraging effect you need to add an explanation or a suggestion. A good rule of thumb is to imagine how you would feel if someone dismissed your efforts or achievement with precisely this remark. A positive approach will pay off with individual children and it can also influence how they treat each other. I have certainly experienced children who have spent time in an encouraging home or group and are happy for each other's achievements with a 'Well done' and 'I like your painting'.

Adults' words are sometimes used beyond request in order to deliver a reprimand: 'I told you not to touch that paint!' You need to keep alert to your level and way of reprimanding children. You will have to speak to children sometimes about what they must not be doing, as hard as you try to keep your communication in a positive frame. It is certainly possible to develop bad habits as an adult, telling children off for minor wrong-doing or keeping up a stream of irritated remarks that create a nagging and unpleasant atmosphere. Continued stress on the adult can lead to such a pattern and it is easier to see this in other adults. Good working relationships between staff in groups will be crucial in finding a tactful way to alert a colleague to this slippery slope.

It can be a sobering experience to hear children telling off their teddies or dolls with the same words and tone that the children have experienced in their turn. Never be cross with a child for this imitation. It is not a form of naughtiness because they are copying familiar adults in this pattern as in many others. If you are uncomfortable by what you hear, and it sounds like you, then monitor yourself from now on. If fierce words and threats are not an imitation of you, then you may need to keep a watch to assess how much a child is taking from an unhappy home life and whether the situation needs intervention from you or more senior colleagues.

Alertness to your own use of speech

It is difficult to become aware of your own use of language during your conversations. You are so involved in what you are saying and in other contributions to the conversation that it is hard to consider your own speech objectively.

There are several ways that you can gain a more detached viewpoint:

- You can certainly keep alert to what you say as you say it, but do not depend only on this method.
- Ask a colleague to observe you for short periods of time and to note down what you say. You could use the methods described on page 44; they are as relevant to observations of adults as well as children. Look over your colleague's notes and perhaps mark up what you have said by the uses of speech. You may be more comfortable if you then observe your colleague and the whole exercise is set positively for you both to assess your use of language in the group.
- You could tape record a session with the children and listen afterwards to what you say and how you say it. You will need a quiet session and a good tape recorder or else it will be hard work listening to the recording.

Your aim is to gain an honest picture of the breadth of your use of language during an ordinary session with the children. You might ask yourself (or discuss with a colleague) the following questions:

- Am I spending time saying 'Don't do that' rather than offering 'Why don't you try this?'
- Am I making empty remarks such as 'That's nice' rather than asking a child about her drawing or the experience she is recounting?
- Do I encourage children to continue with 'Tell me more?' or 'What happened then?'
- Do I extend children with questions like 'What will happen if . . .' and help them to discover and think ahead in a given situation?
- Do I spend time controlling the children when a conversation with them would keep them interested and less difficult for me to handle?
- Do I tend to tell the children the answer when they are puzzled or do I try to guide them or hint so they might discover for themselves? On the other hand, do I sometimes withhold information when it would have been better simply to tell a child?
- When I have to give children instructions do I explain as well?
- Do I have verbal habits, like saying 'Just a minute' a lot or saying 'No' to a child's request before I have listened properly?

Alertness to children's use of speech

It is possible to make very detailed observations of children's speech and to classify what they say according to use. But this approach is unlikely to be practical in a busy nursery or playgroup. You can, however, explore children's use of language in an informal way, as well as encouraging them to stretch themselves, by looking at pictures together.

Some story books have especially eye-catching illustrations or you may have some detailed posters on the wall. Suitable illustrations might be street scenes, shopping or markets, a domestic family scene, a hospital – anything that is well drawn and sufficiently detailed to give children scope for many different kinds of comments. Make sure that you have a broad source of illustrations that reflect the diversity of people within Britain, even if your local area has limited diversity of ethnic groups or cultural backgrounds.

An open way to start is to ask a child 'What can you tell me about the picture?' Ideally you should try this activity with one child at a time, otherwise it is difficult to keep track of what different children are managing. See what the child volunteers with encouragement such as 'Well done' or 'Anything else you can see?' and no direct prompts from you towards particular details. Some children who should be capable of broader use of speech may limit themselves to naming objects in the picture: 'That's a car. A boy. A daddy'. Other children may describe actions but in a vague way: 'They going', 'Boy doing that' or 'Shopping'. Other children may offer more details and other comments with very little prompting from you: 'That's a boy and a girl with their Daddy. They're doing the shopping. The Daddy's got a big bag for the shopping. There's a bus. I go on the bus.'

When you feel that a child is running out of steam then you can offer some prompts, perhaps directing the child's attention towards part of a picture with 'What's going on over here, I wonder?' or 'What's this little boy doing?' You may also be able to stretch the child to think beyond the picture with comments like 'Oh, the baby's trying to grab the biscuits. Do you think she'll get them? . . . What will her Daddy say?' Some children may surprise you once you offer some gentle prompts; they may have assumed that you only wanted naming or one-word answers.

WHEN UNDERSTANDING BREAKS DOWN

Communication between adults is not always trouble-free. Even friends and colleagues who know each other well sometimes fail to understand or mis-understand. Children's level of understanding can be influenced by their broad base of knowledge and you have to take that into account when you are helping them through a confusion.

When children do not understand you

Sometimes it makes sense to give a child a direct answer or an immediate demonstration to support their understanding. Sometimes the most helpful route is to help children to discover for themselves, but self-discovery should not be imposed on children as the only way. Adults have more general knowledge, a broader intellectual framework and a great deal of experience. Sometimes the best route is to share this with children and children who are rarely given a straight answer to a straight question can become very frustrated with adults.

Sometimes it can be hard for adults to grasp what it is that a child does not understand (see also page 75 for the example of learning abstract concepts). You need to listen to a child and sometimes watch what they are doing, or not doing, to take yourself as much into their viewpoint as you can. You need patience and a willingness to step back from what may be very obvious to you, but is not obvious to the child.

Children may fail to understand for a number of reasons. Perhaps they were not attending in the first place. You need to make sure that children are listening and looking and to recapture their attention if it has wandered (see page 67 for more on attention). Some practical steps are:

- You can delay children, by words and touch, so that they listen properly rather than plunging in. Some children need more help in this way than others. For example,
  ADULT   Pick up the . . .
  Child starts picking up objects at random.
  ADULT: Justin, wait a minute. Listen to me. I want you to pick up the lids.
- Children who have become distracted need to have their attention brought back to the original task or request.
  ADULT: Dorcas, please go to the shelf and bring me a tissue.
  Dorcas reaches the shelf but reaches for the first object she sees – a book.
  ADULT: Dorcas, think. What did I ask you to bring me?
  If Dorcas cannot recall then the adult can remind her, without impatience.
- Some games can be repeated if a child has not been watching with care.
  ADULT: Now where did I hid the hat?
  Child shrugs and looks blank.
  ADULT: Well, watch me. I'm going to do it again.

Sometimes children have been paying full attention but they genuinely do not follow what you mean. Perhaps your language has been too complex or includes words that are new to this child, or else you may have introduced an idea which the child has never encountered before. If you have made several requests or suggestions within one long sentence, the child may have become muddled. Young children especially need one idea at a time. The following are some practical suggestions for re-phrasing what you have said.

- Sometimes it helps to repeat a request but emphasising the key words. For example: 'Please put the books on the chair next to the table' does not work and you re-phrase as 'No, Janice. Not on the table. Please put them on the chair that's next to the table.' This type of request would be too difficult for many under-threes who would register either 'chair' or 'table' and not the spatial relationship between the two. You would need to simplify as 'Please put the books on that chair' and support your request by pointing.

- You can re-phrase a request and this may be necessary if you realise that an activity is unfamiliar to a child.

  ADULT: Let's stir up the cake mix now.
  Silence from child and no action.
  ADULT: We stir it with this wooden spoon.
  If the child still does not respond then the adult would demonstrate.

- Sometimes a hint will help. You might start a word for the answer or begin a sentence.

  ADULT: What is a bucket for? (Pause) It can carry w . . .
  Or . . .
  ADULT: What did we do this morning? (Pause) Well first of all we got the shopping basket and then we . . .

- Sometimes it is possible, with some thought, to highlight a particular feature for a child. In this example, the adult is guiding the child towards size.

  ADULT: The marble went in the box, didn't it? So, why can't we get this sponge in? (The box is very small)
  CHILD: 'Cos it's a sponge
  ADULT: You're right that it's a sponge but that's not why it won't go in. Look, I'll cut a bit off. That's still a sponge but now it's fitted into the box. I wonder why?

- Offering possibilities or alternatives can sometimes direct a child without giving the answer completely.

  ADULT: Where did that ball go?
  CHILD: Don't know.
  ADULT: Let's see. Did it go under the table? Or did it go under the chair?

- Sometimes children's understanding is best helped by an example to work as a model.

  ADULT: Can you go to the cupboard and get me another sieve, please?
  Child goes to cupboard but looks bewildered.
  ADULT: Do you know what a sieve is?
  CHILD: No.
  ADULT: Look this is a sieve (holds one up). Please get me another sieve like this one.
  In this situation the adult can also reassure for the future with . . .
  ADULT: Nathan, you can always ask, you know. I'll never be cross just because you don't know something.

- Encouragement to children to expand or clarify their comments is worthwhile if a child has not answered a question fully or has gone off at a tangent.

  ADULT: (pouring hot water onto jelly cubes while children watch) Look, what's happening?
  CHILD: It's jelly.

ADULT: Yes, but what's happening to our cubes that we put in the bowl.

CHILD: They're going away.

ADULT: Yes, they're melting away bit by bit. The hot water is making them melt.

- Part of learning for children is to make links between different experiences so that they can grasp themes in how the world works. You may be able to help a child to draw on a previous experience to make sense of a new situation.

ADULT: Now the spaghetti is hard. How do you think it will feel after it's cooked?

CHILD: Don't know.

ADULT: I'll give you a clue. You remember when we cooked the potatoes. They were hard and then after we cooked them, what did they feel like?

CHILD: They were mushy. We mushed them up.

ADULT: Yes, they were mushy, soft, weren't they. Then we had mashed potato.

CHILD: Are we going to mush the spaghetti?

ADULT: We could, I suppose. That's an idea, David. I'd never thought of mashing up spaghetti. I tell you what, let's just mash a bit. I'm not sure if I'll like it.

Sometimes you can suggest a line of action to a child that will help her to explore and focus on a specific aspect of the activity.

ADULT: How is ice different from water?

CHILD: Don't know.

ADULT: Let's see. You turn over the cup of water into the bowl. Now turn over the ice tray. What's happening?

All of these suggestions are practical and relatively simple; you might say that they are common sense. But like much that seems obvious they may not spring to mind when you are faced with a puzzled or silent child. So it is worth developing the habit of using different strategies to help. Sometimes, as hard as you try, children will still be puzzled or you suspect they have not fully understood. There is no point in pursuing an issue beyond children's interest or ability to attend. Children build up their learning bit by bit and over a period of time, so this opportunity will not be the only time to help the child to learn. Better to move on to something that the child does understand or wants to explore than to risk building a picture of adults who will simply not let something go.

When you do not understand a child

Sometimes, of course, it is the adults who do not follow what a child is trying to communicate. The basic reasons for lack of understanding are very similar to when the confusion flows in the other direction.

Paying attention to children

Sometimes you will have failed to attend properly to a child. Perhaps you were distracted in the middle of what she was saying or you made a wrong assumption about what she was attempting to communicate. Either difficulty is a failure on your part to listen properly and the child deserves an apology and a polite request to tell you again.

Understanding the words
When children are in the early stages of learning a language it is usual for them to have some personal ways of pronouncing words and of putting words together in short phrases. Only familiar adults will grasp the child's meaning since it takes time to tune into a young child. If you are working with under-threes then you will need to assign time and patience to become familiar with individual children's way of communicating.

So long as you share a language and similar accent with a child, then you should not have continued difficulty in understanding three and four-year-olds. If you listen well and still fail to understand the words, then the child may have difficulties in speech that need special attention. It is time to talk with the child's parent and discuss consulting a Speech Therapist. Both you and the parent need to watch that you are perhaps continuing to fill in the gaps and the child's expressive ability in language is not improving as it should.

Understanding the meaning
Sometimes you will understand every word that a child says but you still miss the meaning. The most likely explanation here is that the child is failing to tell you relevant information, since children tend to assume that what they know is shared knowledge with familiar adults. If they are chatting about family life and you are a nursery or playgroup worker, you may not know the people or events about which they want to talk. Parents can experience a similar situation when children talk about nursery at home.

In order to encourage the conversation following the child's interests, you will have to ask questions and invite more information. This exchange can be a pleasant reversal for a child since she knows more than you on this occasion. A friendly relationship with parents will also allow you to expand your knowledge of children's concerns and experiences so you are not as confused next time.

Getting through the lack of understanding
An important step is to admit to a child that you do not understand. Adults are so used to being the ones who know more that they tend to overlook this sensible item of communication. Children will not realise you have failed to understand unless you tell them.

If you listen in to everyday exchanges between adults and children you will notice that when adults do not understand a child they often say 'Pardon?' which invites a repetition but communicates wrongly that the adult has not heard. Children naturally tend to repeat what they have said and the adult is no wiser. The other strategy used by adults is to ask questions such as 'What kind of car?' or 'Was it a girl who did this?' Children tend to switch to trying to answer the adult's questions which may not illuminate the meaning and the initiative moves away from the child as speaker. Adults may also play detective with 'Do you mean that . . .?' or 'Is it this you want . . .?'

The most useful first step is to say 'I don't understand' or 'I don't understand the bit about . . .' You can sometimes home in to help a child to help you in your turn, for instance 'I understand you want the book about the naughty children. I can think of three books like that. Let's look.' You can also invite more information without trying to guess for the children, for example 'I'm not sure what animal you saw in the park. Please tell me some more about it.'

Bilingual children who are learning English can have ideas and experiences that they could easily express to you in their first language but you do not speak that language. It is important that you use a range of positive strategies that show how you respect this child's ability and the work she is undertaking. Many of the approaches already mentioned can help, so long as any of your communication is pitched appropriately for the child's current ability in spoken English. The more you can focus together on tangible objects and definite events, the more you will able to make an accurate judgement of what a child cannot yet express to her own satisfaction. You can also then share words and phrases that will help her next time.

ADULT LANGUAGE AND CHILDREN'S LEARNING

It is important that you keep track of how the children's language skills are extending, along with all the other aspects of their development. However, a focus on the children needs to be in parallel with alertness to the use of language – speaking and listening – of yourself and your colleagues. Children will learn a great deal from what you say and how you say it, but they are also learning patterns of communication, including the crucial listening skills within the environment that you create for them.

6
■

PLANNING FOR CHILDREN'S LEARNING

AN EARLY YEARS CURRICULUM

Planning ahead

In any early years centre it is crucial that the children are happy and safe. But they also need plenty of opportunities to learn and an atmosphere that encourages them to be excited about their learning. Children's time in an early years setting should make a noticeable and positive difference to their development. This is equally true whether you are working in a nursery school for over-threes or an early years centre that will cater for very young children and babies as well.

If your setting is to be of real benefit to the children, then you have to think through in detail the following key questions:

- What do you plan to offer the children in terms of play activities and the daily routine of your nursery?
- How will you check that the range of activities is balanced to support children's whole development? How will you adjust your plans for children of different ages (particularly important if you are working in a day care setting) and abilities (always an issue, but especially if you will be taking children with special needs). In a nutshell, in what ways will your plans promote learning for *all* the children?
- How will you ensure that you notice what children are learning or if children do not seem to be progressing? This concern links with issues of observation and useful record keeping (see Part 1 of the book).

These practical concerns take you straight to adults in the nursery and two further sets of questions:

- How will your staff present the activities to children? How should the adults behave towards the children, in order to support their learning? Plans that look good on paper will not work for children unless staff pay close attention to the children, offer appropriate help and create an encouraging and affectionate atmosphere (see especially Chapter 4).
- How will your nursery inform and involve parents in their children's learning? Your nursery's written policies need to be clear and easily available to parents but conversation is equally important. For instance, if you explain well then parents will under-

stand how you are building up the basis for literacy so that 'proper reading and writing' can follow.

Planning through a curriculum

The ideas underlying an early years curriculum are not new. For many years good practice with young children has been to offer a full range of play activities in order to support children's whole development. Many centre teams have planned ahead by organising play activities around the different areas of children's development. Some centres found a positive approach in following specific themes such as 'our families' and weaving activities into the theme, especially for the older children in an under fives setting.

Effective early years workers have looked carefully at individual children to see what and how they are learning through their play and the extent to which there are problems or confusions for the children that need to be addressed. The most effective plans have used the opportunities of the whole day, including care routines for the younger children, and have not been restricted to those activities which seem to be more obviously 'educational'.

A major difference introduced through an early years curriculum rolling down the ages from the National Curriculum has been the stress on consistency between different early years settings, that they should be working within the same framework. This approach to a planned curriculum has also emphasised observable end results of what children could and should be learning. Although good practice in early years has always stressed the importance of meeting children's individual needs, there has often been uneasiness about looking in detail at specific learning outcomes for children. The concern has been that capturing children's abilities at one time will bury the continuing process of their learning. Some risk undoubtedly exists and children are not well served by an approach that drives them towards very narrow learning goals. However, there is an equivalent risk in focusing too much on the process and resisting any attempt to answer the question of 'What exactly can this child manage?'

The introduction of the inspection scheme has brought a more pointed emphasis on how a nursery's curriculum should support children in learning through the concept of desirable outcomes. A booklet from the School Curriculum and Assessment Authority (see the box on page 98) describes the skills, outlook and kind of behaviour that should be the goals in work with children prior to compulsory school. Children vary considerably so it is expected that some will exceed the goals and others will still be working towards them when they enter reception class.

Any early years setting will have to publish the details of their curriculum. Inspection will establish how far the quality of provision is appropriate for achieving desirable outcomes in different parts of the curriculum. But inspectors will not be assessing individual children.

The School Curriculum and Assessment Authority (SCAA) has produced:
For those who work with children – *Nursery Education: Desirable Outcomes for Children's Learning on Entering Compulsory Education.*
For parents – *A Guide for Parents* and *The Next Steps – Information for Parents.*

You can obtain these by calling the Nursery Education Information Line on 0345 543 345.

At the time of writing (1997) further developments in inspection and the final form of baseline assessment for children entering primary school were under continuing discussion. Although both these developments are closely related to the mid-1990s' debate about the early years curriculum, the whole idea of a planned curriculum for young children exists independently.

LEARNING AND THE EARLY YEARS CURRICULUM

This section on planning your early years curriculum takes the key areas for children's learning from the general headings given in the SCAA booklet. These are developed with examples, including suggestions appropriate to working with children younger than three years. Much of what follows is relevant to very young children and babies, but they cannot be expected to manage well in a group. They need an individual focus that helps them to relate to a small number of familiar children and adults. The aim of this section is to support you as you make more detailed plans.

Workers need to be alert to any different assumptions for boys and girls if stereotypes lead you to have lower expectations for either sex in part of your curriculum. Sometimes adults overlook a lack of verbal fluency in boys or accept a low interest in books and then opportunities are lost for those children. In a similar way, no worker should hold assumptions that girls will have a less natural grasp of maths or science.

Personal and social development

In any early years setting the aim of workers should be to support and encourage children as individuals. Children who lack confidence or who doubt their own worth will have more difficulty in taking advantage of an early years setting and in taking the mild risks that are integral to any learning. During your time with children you should be aiming to support the following kinds of personal development.

An early years curriculum must include the younger children.

A growing sense of self-confidence
- Children will grow in self-confidence, and their sense of self-worth increase if they experience encouragement and a positive approach from adults to their difficulties or mistakes.
- You can encourage less confident children to try and all children to persevere with something they find difficult.
- Children feel appreciated when their work is displayed or later kept safe in a folder as their 'portfolio' of work. Friendly contact with parents may help them to acknowledge the value of young children's early creative efforts rather than to dismiss works as scribbles or messes.

- Acknowledge children's efforts as well as achievement. You can work with the children themselves so that they support one another, rather than indulge in harsh judgements of others to feel better themselves.

Respect for others
- Your aim is that children develop a respect for others and a sense of self-worth that is not dependent on undermining other children or being rude to adults.
- Children learn from what they observe, so a key method in how you deliver your setting's curriculum has to be that you act in the way that you wish children to behave. Showing respect for children does not mean that adults let them have their own way all the time. You show what respect means in practice by paying attention to the youngest children, listening to what children have to say and explaining things to them.
- Early years settings are responsible for the image that they give children of the wider world. Your displays, events and play materials should reflect the cultural backgrounds of not only the children who attend now but also the broader society.
- Children can learn about different belief systems through events such as festivals. This part of the curriculum needs to be balanced with care, otherwise the message can be given that one faith is worthy of more time and attention than others.

The growth of self-care
- Children's confidence is boosted by a realisation that 'I can do this myself' and an encouraging adult will help them to also find pleasure in 'I can nearly do this'.
- A positive approach for young children acknowledges the importance of learning self-care skills. Time is made for showing children, supporting them as they try and celebrating progress.
- Children can be encouraged to take on progressively more of their own care, but adults should not lose sight of the fact that children may still need some help.
- Children often wish to take on responsibilities and many safe opportunities can be created within an early years setting for even the younger ones to help. The details of your curriculum should enable you to value what children can learn through helping out in domestic routines such as mealtimes, taking simple messages and sharing responsibility for care of equipment.

The development of relationships
- Early years settings offer opportunities for children to build relationships with others – adults and children – beyond their immediate family.
- Despite the competing pressures of a group setting, make the most of your time with each individual child. A key worker system within an early years setting will support the development of individual relationships with children and parents. Workers have responsibility, of course, for a group of children and families but you can show how

you value individual children's company and their views, without inappropriately developing favourites.

- Young children and babies especially need a very personal relationship and the staff–child ratios must be such as to enable close contact with continuity of care from workers.
- Workers can help children to get along well with each other, although children themselves will chose who will be a close friend. (Adults need to step in if there is a pattern of rejection because of a child's ethnic group, gender or disabilities – see page 149.) Clear ground rules for the setting and careful adult intervention can help children to learn how to play cooperatively with each other.

Getting along together in a group

- Children can learn the different social skills that are required in a group, rather than in one-to-one relationships. Workers can help so long as they recall that group life can sometimes require adjustments of children. You also need to stand back and be willing to look at what you are asking of children (look, for instance, at page 121 on sharing). Children can be encouraged to play cooperatively by adults' ensuring fair give and take and by organising activities that ask everyone to lend a hand.
- Young children in a group are coming to terms with complex social skills, for instance how to make contact with other children, how to join a group or encourage other children to join them. Workers will have to guide children's learning, and show a good example themselves, in how to handle conflict and minor disagreements.
- Group life can offer opportunities for developing awareness and concern for the needs of others. Again you need to show a good example as an adult, for instance, say 'sorry' if you make a mistake. Children are helped by clear and simple rules in an early years setting and by explanations rather than blunt pronouncements.

Language and literacy

Many opportunities for communication are available throughout the day in any early years setting. Once again, a curriculum that considers children's language development only makes sense when workers are alert to their own communication (see Chapter 5). Children should be learning the wide range of skills that develop from confidence in their spoken language and then the beginnings of understanding the written word.

Every part of the early years curriculum offers the potential to boost children's growing confidence in their spoken language – what they express themselves and how they deal with what is said to them, by adults or other children.

Growing confidence in spoken language

- The early years curriculum for England stresses spoken English since nationwide this is the most prominent language. However, the focus on fluency in English should never undermine respect for the whole language skills of bilingual children. In parts of Wales some children's first language will be Welsh and the later school curriculum reflects this as the first language, rather than English.

- The organisation of play activities and setting routines should give children time to express themselves and adults should be ready to help if children cannot find the words.
- You need to ensure that atmosphere of your setting is calm and not continuously noisy or boisterous. There will be time for loud and lively play but children also need quieter times and quiet corners.
- Support for the language development of very young children and babies will require time and attention to their whole communication. It is especially true for young children that workers need to respond to everything the children want to say through gestures, pointing, expression and words.

Listening and talking

- Workers need to consider children's skills of listening to others as well as expressing themselves. You will need to set a good example yourself by listening carefully, showing an interest and not interrupting.
- You can encourage conversation during any play activity, snack and meal time. 'Show and tell' times can work well for over-threes, when children can individually share an experience or idea, if they wish.
- Supporting children's communication is definitely not something to be limited as a specific activity. For very young children especially, many opportunities will arise through the physical care routines.
- With care, you can help children to express their feelings. You could encourage children to put feelings into words through showing your interest, respect and empathy, when appropriate for sad or confused feelings.

Appreciating the different uses of language

- Children can learn to enjoy and appreciate the many different uses of language through a broad experience of songs, rhymes and simple poems. Such activities can be the opportunity to introduce children to languages other than their own, which may sometimes be the family language of some children in the group.
- Story telling can offer a creative use of language and imagination and be a change from books read aloud to children.
- There are also many opportunities in simple drama and role play: either led by you or developed by the children through a corner and equipment that allows for imaginative play.

Reading and writing

- An early years curriculum must build the basis for writing and reading. Children need to understand the whole idea of a written language and the particular way in which English is written.

- You might be using a rich array of books for children to enjoy on their own or through group story sessions. Very young children need individual time or very small groups; they cannot handle large groups for listening to stories.
- Other examples are the broad possibilities in drawing, pattern making and other creative activities. Use of writing in the centre, for instance on displays and labelling, can complement helping children to become aware of writing outside.

Workers in any early years setting need to be alert to when individual children are ready to start reading and writing, rather than having a fixed idea about appropriate age.

- You can be encouraging children to recognise familiar words in books, displays or the local neighbourhood.
- There is every reason to show children how you are reading the words in a book or on instructions. In this way you show children how you use your literacy skills.
- Early years workers need to understand children's full language skills. For instance, some children may be learning at home the written form of a language that shares neither an alphabet nor the same pattern of writing with English.
- Older children in your setting will be ready to practise linking letters for words with meaning, such as their own name.
- Children can combine their growing literacy and creative abilities in making their own books – perhaps dictating their ideas to an adult and then doing the illustrations.
- If you have the facilities, you can build the groundwork for children to grasp that computers can be used for different kinds of learning and not only for repetitive, quick reaction games.

Mathematics

Children are working their way through a wide range of potentially complex concepts in order to build the basis to mathematical understanding. The play activities in an early years setting can offer children plenty of practical experience and a chance to experiment.

Talking about maths
The skills of communication merge with this area of the curriculum since the opportunity to talk about what they are doing can be essential for children to explore their understanding. You will also need to listen and talk with children if you are to grasp how far their understanding extends currently and any confusions.

Giving information and supporting interest
Use conversations together to offer children the correct words to describe what they see and feel. You can encourage them to observe closely, talk about what they see and

draw tentative conclusions. These are all vital building blocks for children not only to understand maths but to be intrigued rather than uneasy about the topic. (A feeling of uneasiness is far too easy for adults inadvertently to communicate to children when those adults have unhappy memories of learning maths.)

Exploring mathematical ideas
- A wide array of play activities can help children, with adult support, to understand mathematical ideas of shape (two and three-dimensional), position, size and relative size and quantity. Children build their understanding over time through a range of experiences and have the chance to explore in their own way.
- As well as play materials that directly address mathematical concepts, many activities use maths as a resource for the play, for instance use of construction equipment, drawing and shape making. Do not underestimate the potential value of outdoor play since physical games and outdoor equipment can provide a direct experience of relative size and shape or different weights.
- Themes and displays can be used to highlight particular ideas and help children to see links between different kinds of mathematical explorations and ideas.

Understanding number
- In any early years setting you can support children as they are beginning to grasp all the meanings of number. They also have to grasp the different systems for writing numbers and letters.
- You can draw from a range of appropriate books, songs and rhymes. Simple board and card games and playing with large dice are another application of number recognition skills and use of number. Displays and children's artwork can be another context in which to practise writing and using numbers.
- Children need to become familiar with the process of counting and start to understand basic operations such as addition and subtraction. It helps children if these potentially complex ideas are grounded in practical explorations, such as applying numbers for ordinary tasks such as laying the table or sorting out equipment. There are many counting songs and games where numbers are part of the physical actions.

Everyday application of maths
- Children need to grasp the concepts in maths and you will help by recognising the task they face (see page 74 for a reminder of how children can become lost in what seem like straightforward ideas to adults.) But children also understand through applying ideas.
- Practical problem solving using maths can be explored through how to build a particular construction. Early science often also uses practical maths as do cooking activities with weighing or cutting up and sharing out food.
- If you have a computer for children's use you take advantage of the wide array of early maths software packages.

- Local trips to the shops or market can provide a real and practical experience of applying numbers to buy goods and pay for them. Such experience can complement children's explorations in their imaginative play.

Knowledge and understanding of the world

Young children are naturally curious about their world and how it operates. If you work with babies and very young children, your task is to walk a delicate balance between supporting children's curiosity and keeping them safe. Safety continues to be an issue with older children, although the adult task becomes more one of helping children to anticipate and avoid potential risk, through their understanding.

- Helpful adults, both in the early years setting and parents at home, can develop children's interest in the world around them. You are partly following where children's curiosity leads but also introducing new areas, which children cannot explore until you open that perspective.
- There will be many opportunities to open children's understanding beyond their own immediate locale. Activities should be developed with care to avoid any implication that different cultures or life styles are odd or exotic.
- Play activities, trips and books can complement conversations with children that both satisfy their current questions and stimulate their desire to know more.
- Older children can observe, keep records and gather information in scrap books and folders.

A growing perspective of time
- Very young children are largely grounded in the present. They come to develop an understanding of the past as well as the present before they share an adult sense of the passing of time. Children start to build a framework in which broader history will make sense through exploring personal and local history.
- You can involve children, and their families, in projects about the group as babies and in their family life. Children are often fascinated about this very personal approach to the past.
- A sense of times past and memories can be explored by reminiscing through conversation or small projects about what children have done in the recent past, for instance special trips.
- History beyond the last few years often makes more sense to children through exploring the changes in their local environment – history that happened where they now live. Visits to explore local history, perhaps at the library, helps children to understand change in a setting that they directly experience. Visitors to your setting, perhaps parents, can talk about their childhood.

The start to an understanding of geography
- Much like a grasp of history, the meaning of geography as a topic makes sense to

children initially through their own surroundings and by trips to different places that they can personally experience.

- There will be opportunities in exploring the environment local to your setting: a park or common, woodland areas, different buildings and town environments. Although they require organisation, it is worth making trips with children to places unlike their usual surroundings, for instance the seaside for city children or a built-up area for children who live in a rural setting.
- Small-scale environments such as the wild flower area in a local park or the pond on the common can help children to observe geographical features, and early science in a familiar setting. Further exploration can sometimes be through building models and collages of different environments.
- You can select and use suitable videos or television programmes to broaden children's horizons. You may also be able to invite local people, especially parents, to share experiences of other places.

Early science
It is very possible with young children to lay the foundations for basic science through their interest in the natural world and living things.

- There are plenty of opportunities within an early years setting to grow flowers, vegetables and quick-growing items such as cress. Visits to local parks and gardens can build a sense of what grows in which season and a sense of time for how long that growing takes.
- Children can learn about living creatures directly through the care of pets within the setting or bringing in experiences of their family pets. You will be able to create mini-habitats for children to observe, such as a wormery or watching frog spawn turn into frogs.
- Again, local parks or commons or the countryside, if easily available to your setting, can provide further opportunities to observe wildlife and the changes, for instance baby ducks on the pond.
- You can introduce children to science all around them through observations of the weather and the changes of season. Such activities bring with them the opportunity to explore through conversation with children. You can also encourage growing literacy as children make collections, scrapbooks, displays and interest tables.
- You can undertake many basic experiments using natural materials such as sand and water and other simple equipment. Cooking also provides science opportunities because it gives a direct demonstration of materials changing, the properties of different ingredients, singly and if blended together and the effects of heat or cooling.

Physical development

Children's physical skills should never be neglected for the intellectual side to learning. It is not only that children can directly experience topics like maths through physical games. If you support and value children's physical activities you are helping them to experience different interests. You lay the foundation for a more active and healthy life style – many adults have too sedentary a life. Physical activity can also boost children's confidence and their emotional well being.

The large physical movements
- Babies and very young children need a safe indoor environment, suitable equipment and an adult who will play with them, not just sit back uninvolved.
- Mobile children need to continue to develop the larger motor skills of walking, running, climbing, balancing and jumping. They will partly use their skills through exploring any outdoor space but equipment is also important: large outdoor fixed apparatus, bikes and trolleys.
- Children's physical use of indoor and outdoor space will be sometimes directed by their own interests and games. Workers should also be ready to introduce physical games, outdoors and inside, to the children. Parents' concerns about children's outdoor safety has led to considerably less playing outside by children and some can be uncertain about how to use space. You can introduce simple games and show children, if necessary, how to play with skipping ropes, bats and balls.

Fine movements
- Children's ability in improving their skills with fine movements will affect their development in many other areas of the early years curriculum. Children cannot, for example, progress in many aspects of their self-care without a corresponding development in careful coordination of hand and eye. A range of play activities give children a chance to apply and practise fine physical skills. For instance: playing with construction materials, making puzzles, drawing, modelling or sewing.
- Children can also apply physical skills as they learn to manage fastenings on their own clothes and in play with dolls. Helping out in the daily routine gives further opportunities, for example pouring drinks or tidying away little pieces of play equipment.
- Children are also applying physical skills as they use tools in woodwork or needlework, or eat their meals. They handle materials to make something in their creative work through simple needlework, collage or junk modelling.

Creative development

The chance to be creative
- All children can develop creativity, since this quality is the ability to produce something with the flair of originality. Creativity does not require outstanding talent, although some children in your setting may already show a flair for some kind of creative work.
- Children can be supported to explore their own creativity through ideas, for instance

in story telling. Or else the originality might be stimulated through exploring a sequence in play, enjoyment of music or making an eggbox sculpture.
- A positive approach to creative activities can help you to boost children's confidence – everyone can make something and be pleased with the result.

A range of crafts
- Children need space to explore their own methods but your task is also to help them to learn different techniques and use suitable tools safely.
- Children need the chance to experiment and explore the possibilities with different art and craft materials. Your role can be to stimulate interest for the present and hopefully for later years, that children may develop absorbing hobbies.
- Children need access to a wide range of painting, drawing, modelling and other craft activities. Apart from satisfaction in creativity, these activities also provide children with links into early science as they explore texture, colour, shape and form in two and three dimensions. They are also applying their physical skills and using their powers of thought as they plan ahead what they will do and how.
- Creative activities such as clay modelling or collage can also be a very physical experience through the sensation of handling clay or moulding paper. Children have direct experience of feeling through the senses of touch and perhaps smell as well as sight.

Use of the imagination
- A rounded early years curriculum will allow children to develop and follow their imagination and use imaginative skills to consider possibilities. Children may play in a home corner and follow through make-believe sequences with simple props. The same corner may be converted into different settings in which children use their skills of communication to try out roles.
- Different art forms also give scope for children's imagination and build a basis for pleasurable activity in later years. Different kinds of music, dance, drama and story telling all give scope as does the flow of lively conversation.
- There are also opportunities for broadening children's horizons beyond the art, music and dance forms of their own culture and introducing other examples. In an ethnically diverse setting, such activities are a clear statement that you value all the children's backgrounds.
- Imaginative and artistic activities may also be a vehicle for children to express their feelings. It is important not to rush to over-interpret children's drawings or their choices in role play. However, a sensitive early years worker can often see the opportunity to give a child the chance to express strong or confused feelings. Any concerns should be shared in a confidential and respectful way with parents.

MAKING THE CURRICULUM WORK

Familiarity and variety

An early years curriculum provides a framework in which you support and extend children's learning. No curriculum should be viewed as fixed or beyond constructive criticism. You and your colleagues should discuss and review plans at regular intervals and you will always need to check that the implementation of your curriculum is appropriate for all the children attending your setting. The arrival of a child with specific visual disabilities may make you realise that you have organised so far always assuming that children can see clearly.

Even experienced and enthusiastic workers can become stale. You need to think creatively about different ways to use familiar play activities and a variety of routes to helping children to learn the same skills or concepts. Discussion within the staff team can often be a very productive way of generating ideas and breaking what you realise has become a repetitive routine.

Different ideas from the same activity

Taking the example of water play, an activity that most children enjoy, you can explore the many different ways that this natural material can support children's learning.

Children can enjoy water in a large water tray but they also relish the full wet experience of a paddling pool on a warm summer day. Water also comes in bowls, sinks, baths, through wet weather, in parts of buildings such as drains or pipes and in expanses of water such as streams, ponds and reservoirs. Obviously, care is needed as children observe or explore these different sources of water but the possibilities are substantial. Water in some or all of these different contexts can offer ways of learning about:

- movement and speed of water;
- the force and strength of water and water under pressure;
- mixing water with other substances – air and water, hot water and different substances, water and cooking, which materials absorb water and which do not, shrinking, drying out;
- different temperatures and extremes – evaporation and freezing;
- floating and sinking, relative weights and which materials float, creatures that float on water and those that swim in it;
- concepts of full and empty, the process of filling and emptying;
- depth and shallowness, danger and water, keeping safe.

You could probably think of more ways to use water in children's learning. Add your ideas to the list. Another exercise could be to take a different play activity, perhaps a set of wooden bricks, the sand tray, a climbing frame or the home corner and list all the many different ways the same play materials could be used for learning. This type of exercise can also help you if you are working with children who have a narrow range of interests or who are fixed in the play materials that they are willing to explore. Look imaginatively at what the children could learn rather than trying initially to shift them to a completely different activity.

Different routes to learning similar skills or concepts

Another approach is to start from what you would like children to learn and generate a wide range of activities which could support this learning.

The example of spatial relationships

For instance, learning about movement and spatial relationships can be built through indoor activities such as building materials, farmyards and small scale animals, cars and a roadway mat, play materials that fit together and doll's house size people and equipment. All these materials are also supportive, obviously, of other skills, for instance in imaginative play for children. Ideas of space, movement and the words to describe them can also be developed in physically active play and outdoor activities. You might organise music and movement, a game of imitating the movements of a leader or moving according to instructions (sidewards, backwards, close together, finger-tip distance apart) or simple obstacle courses on foot or bikes where children experience in their whole body movements the meaning of 'through', 'under' or 'over.

The example of understanding of time

Early mathematical ideas can be approached through a range of activities and you will help children so long as you appreciate the complexity of what they are learning and that understanding takes time to build. For instance, few children who start primary school have a confident grasp of time as read from a clock or watch but they can have built an understanding of time passing and a general concept of time.

Exploring a sequence in a story or a series of related pictures is one early stage in grasping time and time passing. Children often like to recount a tale or to go back over an interesting morning with, 'First we . . ., then we . . . and last of all . . .' A set of pictures can tell a tale and children have to sort out the sequence and then talk about the story shown in the illustrations. Older children may like the challenge of two sets mixed up together which have to be sorted.

Ordinary daily activities help children to understand times of the day and the passing of time. Day or sessional facilities have a routine which, so long as it does not become an imposition on adults and children, can be a positive way of helping children to grasp what follows what. Drink, snacks or lunch will arrive at a predictable time, tidying up has to be complete before lunch, parents will arrive at a similar time each day or end of session. Children will initially learn about time through activities that make sense to them. Long before they will really understand 'We have ten minutes before tidy up time', they will follow 'You have time to do one more painting, if you want'.

Adults can also be helpful in watching their own language about time. You might note through observation that adults, including yourself, are lax in the use of phrases like 'I'll just be a minute' or 'I won't be long'. Children survive these inaccuracies but do not be surprised if they develop a cynical attitude to the meaning of 'a few minutes'.

Children can learn to distinguish days of the week if something special happens each day. Monday might be the day you water the indoor plants or rearrange the nature table. Tuesday might be the lunch time for watching a special television programme. You do not have to organise a rigid day-by-day timetable but a few fixed activities can be helpful. In conversations with children you can encourage the use and understanding of 'yesterday', ' last night', 'tomorrow' or 'in two weeks' time'. Longer stretches of time, perhaps to a special trip, could be counted down on a calendar with the days marked.

GOOD PRACTICE AND AN EARLY YEARS CURRICULUM

For some time now it has been good practice in early years to have clear plans in your work with children. The concept of an early years curriculum gives shape and consistency to your plans. Any framework will always have to be applied with attention to the individuality of children and an alertness to checking assumptions within your staff team. If your setting includes very young children and babies, then a broad framework applicable for older children has to be adjusted towards the different understanding of the very young and their need for a very personal approach.

SUGGESTED FURTHER READING

Derman-Sparks, Louise (1989) *Anti-Bias Curriculum: Tools for Empowering Young Children* (available from Community Insight, The Pembroke Centre, Cheney Manor, Swindon, Wiltshire, SN2 2PQ).

Donaldson, Margaret (1980) *Children's Minds* (Fontana).

Goldschmied, Elinor and Jackson, Sonia (1994) *People Under Three – Young Children in Day Care* (Routledge).

Grieve, Robert and Hughes, Martin (1990) *Understanding Children* (Blackwell).

Hall, Nigel and Martello, Julie (eds) (1996) *Listening to Children Think: Exploring Talk in the Early Years* (Hodder & Stoughton).

Karmiloff-Smith, Annette (1994) *Baby It's You* (Ebury).

Melville, Sandra (1994) *Gender Matters: A Guide to Gender Issues and Children's Play* (Playboard).

Neaum, Sally and Tallack, Jill (1997) *Good Practice in Implementing the Pre-School Curriculum* (Stanley Thornes).

Petrie, Pat (1996) *Communicating with Children and Adults: Interpersonal Skills for Early Years and Playwork* (Edward Arnold).

Pre-School Learning Alliance (1997) *What Children Learn in Playgroup* and (1996) *Equal Chances*.

Quilliam, Susan (1994) *Child Watching: A Parent's Guide to Children's Body Language* (Ward Lock).

Tizard, Barbara and Hughes, Martin (1984) *Young Children Learning – Talking and Thinking at Home and at School* (Fontana).

Whitehead, Marian (1996) *The Development of Language and Literacy* (Hodder & Stoughton).

PART 3

A POSITIVE APPROACH TO CHILDREN'S BEHAVIOUR

7
■

CHILDREN'S UNDERSTANDING AND THEIR BEHAVIOUR

As children are advancing in physical development and language so they are also changing in their emotional understanding and development. Their views of the world and of relationships between themselves and others are developing. Children's ability to recognise and cope with their emotions progresses, as does their understanding of social behaviour such as sharing with others or the concept of danger – two areas which can be important in adults' views of what is 'good' and 'bad' behaviour. All caring adults need to be aware of what are reasonable expectations of children, otherwise the adult judgements of children as 'naughty' or 'they really should have understood that . . .' may take little account of the limited understanding of younger children. Your relationship with children is ideally one of continual and steady adjustments as they learn more about themselves and others.

A sensitivity to children as individuals is as important in early years workers as for parents. This chapter, and the others in Part 3, take a broad framework – early years settings and family situations – since you may be supporting parents in dealing with their own children as much as developing relationships yourself with the children.

THE PERSPECTIVE OF VERY YOUNG CHILDREN

The individuality of babies

Babies are unique individuals as much as toddlers, four-year-olds or school-age children. The differences are there to be seen from the earliest days by anyone who spends time with babies and looks closely, rather than blandly assuming that all babies are much the same.

Some babies are quieter than others, some seem to be more responsive or more wakeful. Some babies seem very jumpy, some get upset more easily and some certainly cry more than others. Even if you are very skilled in the care of babies, each individual will be a new experience because you have not known this particular baby.

Match and mismatch
Since a baby's individuality is present from the early days and weeks, then the match between adult and child is central to making life easier and more pleasant. For instance, if your preferred way of handling a baby is through plenty of games and movement from the start, then a baby who enjoys action and being carried about will fit more

easily with your style. If a baby is very sensitive and happier with slow, gentle handling, then you need to adjust your approach. If a parent or other carer believes that young babies should be quiet and content in a cot or pram for much of a day, then a very peaceful baby will suit. Another adult might be disappointed in what appears to be a lack of responsiveness in the baby. Babies vary and so do adults and the combination is a unique one each time.

If you are the primary carer you will sometimes have to adjust your preferred style. Alternatively you might be supporting a parent whose firm views, or perhaps those of a grandparent, do not fit this individual baby. You might also on occasion have to intervene through concern. For instance, an extremely quiet baby is not 'good', there could be cause for worry. Babies should not naturally be passive and silent and those that sleep very many hours without waking may not be getting enough feeds in a day.

Adults' needs in perspective

Caring for babies and very young children is demanding and tiring. Even adults who really enjoy being a parent or early years worker have days when patience and understanding run low. A focus on adult sensitivity to babies is not a denial of adult feelings and wishes. It is rather that with many adults the balance is too much in the other direction. Care of babies can be more enjoyable and less stressful if they are given respect for their needs and wants.

A good example of seeking a balance is that many adults expect that babies will tolerate being handed around from lap to lap and should even welcome the sudden attentions of complete strangers. Most adults would be most disconcerted if a stranger came up very close and tried to touch them or grinned directly into their face. Babies are not adults but they also dislike sudden intrusions into their personal world. By six or seven months babies will express clear preferences about contact with familiar or unfamiliar adults and protest about unwelcome contact or unfamiliar handling.

As babies become toddlers, adult needs for affection sometimes take the form of expecting a child to be pleased to see them, perhaps when a parent picks up a child from day nursery or a grandparent arrives for a visit. Yet children's reactions vary and do not always match what an adult hopes. Sometimes young children want time to settle and react poorly to demands to express affection. As children become older some parents require gratitude 'for all I've done for her!' Again this demand is a solely adult perspective and rarely brings the required reaction. Of course, there are times when adult and child wishes for affection or attention coincide and these can be joyful times.

A sense of security for children

By the first birthday children who have experienced a manageable number of familiar adults will clearly show their attachment to those people by wanting them in sight or hearing for much of their waking hours. The reassurance of a familiar face or voice is often necessary, even if the child seems absorbed in play. The frustrations of the second year of life also need the reassurance of a caring adult nearby for comfort in times of upset and help in play. Parents and other carers have to accept that very young children will not play on their own for long periods of time so adults do not have uninterrupted stretches to themselves. This need for the time and attention of an adult does not mean that a very young child is 'spoiled' or is being 'demanding'; it is a very natural state for young children and important for their development. Children learn to venture a little on their own if they have confidence that adult attention, help and encouragement are there for the asking.

The rising twos can be emotionally dependent on adults and their behaviour may swing from one extreme to another. They want to cling to a familiar adult in times of worry or stress but on other occasions may fiercely demand to be allowed to do something without help. Such swift changes can be confusing especially if adults are not aware that such apparent inconsistencies are very usual for this age group. The young children are not being inconsistent from their perspective.

For example:

Danielle wants to talk with a friend without interruptions from 18-month-old Ronny but he is unsure of his surroundings in the friend's home and wants his mother's familiar attention before he is at all willing to 'go and play', especially with the friend's two-year-old daughter who has already given Ronny a good shove. Later in the day, back at home, Ronny is fully at ease and well occupied with emptying out the interesting waste bin. His mother moves in to protect him from the bin's contents and he throws a fierce tantrum. Earlier he wanted her protection but now he sees it as interference.

LOOKING THROUGH CHILDREN'S EYES

Being able to play 'properly'

Children's behaviour in their play reflects their personality and experience. Individual children may always vary in how much they prefer to play alone and how much in the company of others. But, patterns of play are also shaped by children's level of understanding at different ages.

It used to be said that children under two did not play cooperatively, but tended more to play alongside one another – parallel play. The real picture is more subtle than this

Your expectations have to be appropriate for the age of the children.

description. Observational research of very young children shows that they do make contact with their peers, form attachments to other children and take part in shared activities, even though these may not last long and often need the support of an adult. Play also develops across the ages. Older children, for instance in a family home, will sometimes make space for a younger sibling to become part of a game. Younger children then become a part of play sequences, sometimes special to these individuals, that they would not have initiated on their own. Younger children are often very interested in the activities of older children. They may just want to watch but, frustratingly for the older ones, the interest sometimes moves into carrying off some of their toys.

Young children, under two years, enjoy imitating the actions of older children and adults. In a specialised setting such as a nursery many of the ordinary dangers have been removed. In a family home, the limited understanding of this age group can make life worrying and frustrating for parents, especially if they do not learn to see the world at least sometimes from children's perspective. Very young children cannot understand that it is all right to paint on walls that are being redecorated but not to crayon on walls in general. The child's ability is not yet matched by an understanding of 'It's only all right if . . .'

The understanding of danger

Two-year-olds have learned so much that you can be surprised sometimes at the large gaps that exist, and will exist for some time, between a child's and an adult's view of the world. Especially when a child has well-developed language, you may expect too mature a level of understanding.

Children are naturally curious and this helps their learning but a sense of danger does not really develop until closer to three years. The physical abilities of two-year-olds carry them into potential trouble with devastating speed. At home or at nursery, young children learn that certain actions are not permitted or that specific items, like scissors, are only allowed if they are the child's own version. Children learn to cooperate, especially if the limits are made with consideration, but they have only a limited grasp that the prohibitions are because of potential harm to themselves or others.

It simply does not occur to young children that they might be physically hurt as a consequence of what they are planning or currently doing. Think back to your own childhood; you almost certainly had some games and play places that you realise now were risky. Often it seems children's inability to see danger in climbing a rickety tree have meant that their climbing remained safe because they were not anxious. Children, not the very young, usually have some sense of self-preservation and, unless urged on by others, often stop at what feels like a safe stage.

Young children – the under-fives and especially the under-threes – need to be protected from their very limited understanding of consequences. It is not fair to get angry with young children; explanations like 'But you might fall over and hurt yourself' mean very little. If a child has a mild fall then this experience may add to her understanding but accept that the hurt she feels may blot out the lesson. It is not fair either to indulge in 'I told you so'. Hurt or shaken children need comfort and not criticism and a gentle pointer to what happened will be more effective than adult crowing.

Even children of school age can feel frustrated by adults who see potential danger where the children see none. With older children, for instance, in an after school or holiday club, you have to walk a middle course of trusting children to keep to sensible limits and stepping in if you feel there is danger. Your involvement, for instance when crossing roads or handling tools, can be part of teaching children how to take care. It should never be a straight leap with children from 'No you mustn't' to 'You can do it on your own'.

The hurt and upset of others

It is important to teach toddlers not to lash out or bite. Yet they have limited understanding of another's pain and can be puzzled by appeals to think about others, especially if an adult goes on and on. Young children also tend to be overwhelmed by the emotion of the moment and it takes time before they learn to hold back from a physical response to frustration or distress.

Helping children to develop empathy
In the short term, young children learn that parents and other carers disapprove of slapping or biting and that the child who receives most attention after such an incident is the one who has been hurt. In the longer term, children can develop empathy: the ability to tune into the feelings of others and to respond sensitively to their emotional needs. Even two- to three-year-olds, when they are not themselves in distress, will sometimes move to comfort another child who is upset. By four or five years and older, children can be very concerned about the upset of a friend or a familiar adult and may try to help.

This development of an altruistic outlook does not emerge just because the years have passed; it appears to be the consequence of a particular pattern of behaviour from parents or other carers in a child's life. If you want to support children to develop an altruistic outlook, an important first step is to create an affectionate and warm atmosphere – in a family home or early years setting. The other ways of encouraging altruism all have implications for how the adults behave:

- Set clear rules for children's behaviour and apply them consistently. Explain the reason for a rule in terms of its consequences. A general rule like 'You mustn't hit people' is supported by a short and specific explanation that 'When you hit Dave, you hurt him.' Avoid the negative approach of trying to induce guilt feelings with comments like, 'Don't you think that was a nasty thing to do!'

- Create opportunities for children, even young ones, to do helpful things. Encourage them to help but do not insist or try to make them feel guilty if they do not.
- Perhaps most important of all, behave in the way that you wish children to behave – show that you consider the feelings of others, that you look through the children's eyes.

A perspective on time

Babies live in the present and toddlers' time perspective only stretches a little either side. Children under two years show that they remember and learn from experience but there are gaps. They can recall where toys or biscuits are kept or how to open the cupboard door. But this reference back to past is firmly rooted in the needs and wants of the present. The wishes of the moment can also over-rule experience. For instance, a toddler may have become adept at walking around a low table. Then one day her eyes and mind are firmly on reaching a favourite toy before another child and she runs straight into the edge of the table.

Two- and three-year-olds have limited speech to talk about past or future events and adults have to allow for this. There is little point in telling children 'But you promised this morning' because it is no longer this morning and a young child does not really understand the concept of a promise. Four- and five-year-olds have a much broader grasp of the past and plans for the future but this understanding is still growing – listen to a few five-year-olds talking about what happened 'a long time ago'.

Waiting
Two-year-olds have a very limited ability to 'wait until later', or for the elastic adult description of 'in a minute'. From the perspective of a very young child, what is worth having should be had now. If you are patient and focus on the child you can help him to be more flexible, to wait for a specific time ('I must finish changing the baby, then I will get your book') or to accept an alternative. But an acceptable alternative is unlikely to be waiting quietly while you finish a long task or several, or standing by while another child dominates the favourite plaything. Three-year-olds can have learned to wait so long as they have positive experiences that reassure them that adult promises, such as 'You can have the bike when Jamal has finished' are honoured. Children whose experience is that waiting means not getting have no incentive to postpone their immediate wishes.

Understanding sharing

Children can learn to share and to understand what adults mean by this word but it is equally important that adults understand the situation. Sharing is a pattern of behaviour that makes group life more harmonious, yet 'you must learn to share' is required by many adults without a clear vision of what they are really asking.

An ability to look towards the future is important in learning to share. A two-year-old cannot genuinely share and it is pointless to expect this behaviour from them. Very young children may hand over a toy on request and the adults may then give it to another child. Or else young children may cooperate in swopping playthings. With appropriate experience, children learn steadily the difference between their own and others' possessions, that their own are returned and that group possessions, in nursery or playgroup, can be enjoyed by everyone but belong to no individual.

Three- and four-year-olds can have learned to share but, like any pattern of behaviour, sharing does not appear automatically with age. If children's experience is that their own possessions 'shared' with others are not returned or are broken, then they will learn to resist adult requests to share. In order to comprehend the child's position, you should really imagine a possession of your own, that you care about as much as the child cares about this picture book or the bright red bus. Think: would you hand over your favourite jacket or new CD to a relative stranger visiting your home or a friend whom you knew to be careless?

Children can learn the give and take that makes group life happier if they get their turn. If children find that the nursery bikes are used mainly by children rough enough to resist attempts to get a turn, then the less forceful children may hold onto those playthings that they can. If the associations of sharing are unpleasant no child will voluntarily share.

What are you really asking?
There are three types of behaviour that adults ask of children which are distinct but all are called 'sharing'.

1 Children are asked to share their toys when other children come to play at home, or with their siblings. The rules are, or should be, that the toys are returned to the owner, so adults are really asking here that children 'lend' and 'borrow'.
2 In a group children are asked to share toys that belong to the nursery or playgroup, so they are being asked here to 'take turns'.
3 A third way in which adults use 'share' is when children are asked, 'Share your crisps with the other children'. Crisps, or sweets, are a one-time possession and are not returned, so children are here being asked to 'give'.

Any of these behaviours are fair to ask of children, so long as adults are behaving sensibly (see the provisos earlier in the section) and recognise that children are being asked a lot. They will learn with support but negative pressuring of 'You must learn to share' or 'Don't be so selfish – share!' are unlikely to encourage spontaneous sharing.

Are you asking too much?

By three and four years of age children's emotional and social development has progressed to a point where they can behave, some of the time, more in line with adults' views of 'good' behaviour. Three-year-olds are more able to play together and resolve some of the difficulties that arise. They can and are willing to cooperate and may enjoy helping others. They have some sensitivity to the feelings of others. But children will not behave in this way all the time. If they are tired, ill or at the end of a hard day then they will not be on their best behaviour and will need comfort not annoyance from parents or other carers. Remember that adults, although capable of patience, altruism, cooperation or courtesy do not behave like that all the time, so do not expect standards from children that you know are met by very few adults.

THE CULTURAL CONTEXT

Much of children's learning in the early years and the work of adults is towards encouraging behaviour which the adults believe is acceptable within the family and the immediate social world. Adults vary considerably in the details of what they judge to be appropriate behaviour and there are wide differences between and within cultures.

Babies learn the mealtime behaviour and sleep patterns of their adult family members. For example, in Britain, children are trained out of an afternoon nap but in hotter climates everyone may plan their day around an afternoon siesta. Children learn the ways of behaving which are more or less acceptable to the adult community in which they are raised. In British schools we stress the importance of time limits on many activities, of asking questions of the teacher and in producing your own work unless cooperation is specifically allowed. In some other cultures such ground rules would be incomprehensible, since it would be rude to question an older person or one in authority and strange to stop a piece of work because time was up rather than that you had done the best job possible.

Babies and children learn the social codes of their culture and immediate social group. They do not learn them perfectly or else they may learn and prefer different patterns of behaviour that disrupt home or school.

The importance of adults

Within a single culture there will be differences in how adults react to children and you have to be cautious about making generalisations to a whole culture or community on the basis of a few known families. However, a consistent theme is that children's social and emotional development depends upon learning and therefore on experiences. The appearance of patterns of sharing or the passing of tantrums do not happen automatically. Such changes are influenced by how parents and other carers treat children. This is the reason you will find at least as much emphasis in the following chapters on adults' behaviour as on children's.

8

A FOCUS ON HOW ADULTS BEHAVE

CHILDREN LEARN FROM EXPERIENCE

Children learn from people around them as their models, from the experiences of what happens to them day by day and the sense that they make of events. Children react to the behaviour of others – adults and other children – and learn from the limits imposed and what seems to be approved behaviour. The process of learning is not fully intentional in the way that children could explain why they have done or not done something, but then often adults cannot give a very coherent explanation of their own actions and intentions.

Children have also learned about what kind of behaviour seems to work, to achieve a desired goal. The end result, in terms of how children behave, does not always appear to an onlooker to be very sensible. But behaviour that surprises or irritates others is often achieving a goal for the individual concerned. There may, of course, be other ways of reaching this goal which avoid the irritation.

Individuality

The end results can be very different even for individuals who appear to have had similar experiences, for instance siblings in the same family. Children are dissimilar partly because even siblings are often treated differently and older children have different experience because of the birth order. The impact of experience is also filtered through any child's individuality. Babies show differences in their reactions and responsiveness from the early weeks and adults who care for them behave differently. There is an interaction. (See also the idea of match and mis-match on page 115.)

Children's individuality colours their reactions but does not make them fixed in their behaviour. Just as they learn ways of behaving, so they can shift their patterns and develop subtleties, such as reacting differently to adults, even within the family, depending on those adults' behaviour. Children may seem fixed in their behaviour largely because people and circumstances have combined in such a way that there is limited incentive to change.

Similar feelings may emerge in different ways with different children. There are, for example, a variety of ways for angry feelings to be expressed. Some children, from a combination of personality and the model they have observed from adults, will express anger fiercely outwards with strong words and physical actions, perhaps hurting others. Some children may feel equally strongly but are able to express themselves in words

> **For example:**
>
> Finn has learned from previous experience that threatening or actually attacking younger children brings an adult running. A dramatic situation develops and Finn feels at the centre of the action. The fact that adults are cross with him counts for little when set against their full attention. Finn has learned to be satisfied with an angry and focused adult. He is unlikely to change unless the key adults in his life make a deliberate attempt to reduce the dramatic consequences of Finn's attacks and give him regular experience of a different kind of attention from adults.

and perhaps to let the feelings out before they get to an explosive level. Some children turn strong feelings inwards, perhaps feeling anxious that they have such angry thoughts, and may hurt themselves or become very miserable if they are not helped to express what they feel.

Expectations on gender

Many adults treat boys and girls differently, in subtle and not so subtle ways. Good practice in early years has become established as encouraging equal opportunities for the two sexes, but you need to recall that this approach is contrary to some families' beliefs. Some cultures, including traditions in Britain, support a stance that raising children appropriately directs girls and boys towards different patterns of behaviour and aspirations. Some parents will be happy to adjust or recognise the disadvantages of an unequal approach. Some will continue to disagree.

Certain kinds of behaviour tend to be encouraged for boys and not girls, and vice versa. Boys are often allowed to be noisier and play more roughly than girls before an adult steps in. Boys may be allowed to have an untidy room at home with the almost admiring excuse of 'he's a real boy'. Rigid divisions can cut across children's interests and their feelings. A young boy and girl may be equally sensitive and moved by the plight of others. The girl may be allowed to cry in sympathy or to help but the boy may be discouraged with 'Big boys don't cry' or criticised for being 'soft'. He may learn to hide his feelings, perhaps cover them up with a show of bravado. Alternatively he may be unable to stem his tears and come to see himself in a negative way if the adults around do not value male gentleness.

Flexibility

People who feel strongly that personality determines behaviour and outlooks on life are likely to judge there is little hope in changing anybody. They may excuse themselves with 'You have to forgive me. I can't get anywhere on time' or make rigid judgements about children such as 'You'll never change her. She's an evil-tempered little cow.'

People's personality, the core of what makes them an individual, is unlikely to change and is best seen as a given. Attitudes are also very resistant to change, although some people are more flexible than others. However, the way that personality and attitudes are expressed through behaviour is much more amenable to change. Children are also potentially more flexible than adults, who can be very set in their ways.

A POSITIVE AND REALISTIC FRAMEWORK

Approaches rather than solutions

In dealing with children there is rarely, if ever, a perfect match between a problem arising from their behaviour and something specific that adults can do as an effective solution. Understandably, you often hope for an easy answer and some difficulties with children are resolved with less effort than others. The idea that there are neat answers is perpetuated by adults who are wise away from the main action, making comments like 'It's too late now, of course, but what you should have done with her was . . .' or 'It's all because you would keep picking him up when he cried as a baby.'

The fact that much of this so-called advice is after the event only adds to the unhelpfulness. There is no way of knowing whether the answer offered with such confidence now would have worked like magic. In reality simple suggestions for dealing positively with children's behaviour usually imply some change in the behaviour of adults but not a simple one-off solution – 'You do this and then she won't do that anymore.'

FOCUS ON ADULTS – NOT BLAME

Adults' feelings and actions are a major influence on children and so attention has to be paid to that side of any interaction with children. Adults should also be able to take a broader perspective and a longer-term view than young children. You are more able to consider your feelings in a moment of calmness and to behave differently towards a child in a deliberate pattern. The stress is on 'more able' and not 'always able' because adults can become stressed too and can be so involved in a difficulty with a child that it is hard to think objectively. A colleague or friend who will listen can be a useful sounding board and be able, without blame, to point you towards how you could change the situation for the better with a child. There is no fairness in blaming a child for everything but neither is it fair to heap criticism on yourself, or other adults. Everyone has to deal with the situation as it is now and not with what might have happened if anyone had behaved differently in the past. These 'if only's' get everyone nowhere fast. Look also at page 193 for help in the conversation when you are discussing this kind of situation with a parent.

Change may take time

You have to be prepared to persevere in dealing with children, especially if they have learned to behave in a way that is driving everyone to distraction. There is no need to take the defeatist attitude of 'It's too late now, she's so set in her ways'. Undoubtedly, the longer the situation has continued, the harder it may be to change her behaviour, but it is not impossible and you may have to tolerate that her behaviour gets worse before it improves. But sometimes children respond positively and quickly to a new adult with a firm and different approach.

For example:

Three-year-old Jasmine has learned from her family experience that whining and complaining, followed by throwing things, breaks down her mother's resistance and 'No, you can't' is changed into 'All right then'. Annop, her key worker at the Mandela Children's Centre, has taken a firm yet affectionate line with Jasmine and she no longer behaves in this way at the centre. Annop is supporting Angela, Jasmine's mother, who really wants to change the miserable situation at home and enjoy life more with her daughter. Annop warned Angela that Jasmine would most likely get worse before there was any improvement, because the child needed to believe that Angela had changed her approach. Annop's prediction was correct and he offered a great deal of support to Angela to persevere, hold consistently to a 'No' that mattered, be flexible on less important issues and work hard to encourage Jasmine.

It's just a phase

Some difficult times with children can be seen as part of their normal development. A common example is the ease with which under twos, and even under-threes can slip into a temper tantrum. At this young age, an emerging sense of self and clear ideas of what they want to do are combined with limited ability to express frustrations in words or to re-direct themselves once children have worked themselves into a state. So two-year-old tantrums can be called a phase and the knowledge that outbursts are not unusual with young children can be a comfort to an embarrassed or fraught parent. However, this knowledge does not solve the immediate situation, such as having to deal with a kicking, screaming bundle of fury, and often in front of other people (see page

151 for some ideas). So saying a pattern of behaviour is a developmental phase is useful, but only up to a point.

CONSISTENCY IN ADULT BEHAVIOUR

Being consistent over your own rules

Children are learning from the model of adult behaviour that they observe. Children who experience key adults who are inconsistent will see no point in keeping promises themselves or in co-operating with an adult who may change the rules tomorrow. Inconsistency from adults confuses children. Instead of learning about limits to what is allowed and the circumstances under which some rules may be flexible, children learn that adults are generally unpredictable or can be swayed.

For instance, it is hard for a child to understand what parents want if sometimes cheekiness is seen as amusing and then later the parents punishes the same clowning around that was treated as a joke the day before. Parents may claim they have their reasons, for instance that 'It was all right yesterday as we were at home, but today she showed me up in front of the doctor' or simply 'I wasn't in the mood today'. Children can learn that different behaviour is required under different circumstances, perhaps some kinds of joke are just for within the family or that a parent feels ill today and need peace. However, these changes need to be explained and adults have to appreciate that for younger children the change-about will make no sense – except that the adult has been unfair.

Consistency is especially important when dealing with children who are proving difficult to handle. The child needs to grasp that clear consequences follow on from certain kinds of behaviour which the adults are working to discourage. If the ground rules vary, then children are far less likely to change how they behave and more likely to push against unclear boundaries between what is and is not allowed. If children learn that sometimes an adult can be nagged or bullied into giving way on what has been presented as a hard and fast rule, then they will try resisting in the future.

Consistency between adults

Consistent patterns are also important between different adults dealing with the same children – within a family or in an early years group. Inconsistency can be especially disruptive when a child is already hard to handle. Perhaps a child has only to reach a low level of aggressive behaviour before one adult steps in but can become very aggressive before a second adult intervenes. When children are pushing adults to the very limits, it is essential that adults – workers or parents – discuss together and reach an agreement on how everyone should deal with the child and the exact limits (see the examples on pages 14 and 54). This discussion should happen out of the child's hearing, especially if there is disagreement between the adults.

It is preferable that family life and out-of-home care, whether a nursery or child minder, should be consistent on major principles but it is not realistic to seek 100% consistency. Adults vary in many small ways in how they feel comfortable in dealing with young children. The children in turn learn that slightly different rules operate at home and at their grandparents' house. Home and playgroup will be different places. So long as individuals are consistent within their own rules, children will learn the reality that people differ. However, if the variation is significant then there may be some confusion.

Very different views on dealing with the same child can lead to antagonism between the adults. Perhaps a worker's view is that 'I spend all week toilet-training him in nursery and his parents don't bother at the weekend. So it's back to square one on Monday.' Yet, in another situation, a parent might object with 'She plays very happily at home, so how can you say she's such a pest at playgroup!' Neither of these conflicts are the child's problem; the adults concerned have to sort things out. A calm discussion is needed about timing and methods in toilet training – perhaps the parent has not been consulted about a suitable age to start or genuinely believed that the worker wanted to do this alone. In the second example, perhaps this child plays contentedly in a home where an adult is close by to help and become involved. However, the playgroup has developed into a noisy and demanding environment and this child has judged correctly that only serious pestering will get an adult's attention.

Children easily learn different ways of behaving at the meal table, in line with the expectations and habits of the different adults. The concern of 'She eats her lunch for you at nursery but she won't eat for me' is again not the child's problem, although it may seen in terms of her 'naughtiness'. Perhaps she has learned how mealtimes work differently at home and nursery and she is conforming on the basis of experience. If her parent wants an easier meal time then perhaps there is something to learn from nursery: a social atmosphere at the table and not seeing rejection of food as lack of affection for the adults.

LOOKING FOR ALTERNATIVES

The possibility of diverting children

Adults do not have to stand by waiting for a situation to worsen. Some adults cannot be bothered to anticipate difficulties and sit back with a self-satisfied, 'There he goes again!' or call 'Stop it!' ineffectively from a distance. Sometimes an alert and well-placed adult may be able to divert a child from an aggressive attack or from hurting herself. Distractions do not always work, of course, but they are effective often enough to make them worth being high on your list of possibilities.

It can be hard work to spread yourself between the children.

Your success in diverting children from one course of action into another depends on knowledge of individuals. Some children may be distracted from fights over the favourite bike by being offered another outdoor toy which the adult knows is highly prized. Sometimes the invitation to 'Come and help me' may be a tempting prospect. A patient adult may be able to show two children how to rearrange an activity so that they can both have an equal part. At other times an effective diversion from the troubles can be the request to 'Tell me what's happened here'. This role of referee and general releaser of tensions is usually for adults – children can only sometimes do it for themselves.

Offer a choice

Another way to divert children from a troublesome course of action is to offer them a choice between two alternatives. You have to be careful not to over-use this approach, otherwise the novelty of choosing is lost. Rising twos and two-year-olds who have developed firm ideas can sometimes be distracted by a choice. When my son was nearly two years old, his demands for a biscuit could sometimes be side-tracked by an offer of 'No biscuit. You can have a carrot or raisins'. He would then ponder the choice between two snacks that he enjoyed and would often happily pick one of those. Older children may more readily accept that they cannot go on a local trip today if an attractive choice is offered for what they might do indoors.

Encouraging a particular alternative

With some kinds of behaviour that adults wish to discourage, there is a specific alternative action that literally cannot happen at the same time. The two ways of behaving are incompatible. (See the boxed example below.)

For example:

In Queensmere Nursery, two-year-old Erin has developed the habit of throwing food at mealtimes and sometimes toys at other times. Her key worker, Harriet, is trying to encourage Erin into a giving action, which is incompatible with the throwing. Initially, Harriet has been making most of the effort to create a giving action, by catching Erin's hand as she moves to throw, gently guiding her to give or to place a spoon of food back on the plate or a toy on the table surface. Harriet then says 'Thank you, Erin' in a lively way that she knows Erin likes. When she fails to catch Erin in time, Harriet says a firm 'No Erin, no throwing food' but does not shout at the child. Erin has now become intrigued with the giving game and throws much less. Harriet is also spending time to expand Erin's interests in play.

Looking for incompatible actions can be a constructive approach. A child cannot bite and kiss at the same time, cannot be patient and impatient with a younger child. The incompatible alternative may not be an easy action to encourage but the approach can help you to focus on what behaviour you would like to see from this child, rather than focusing only on the negative. The result of a more positive orientation may be that you realise the child does show patience sometimes or shows a flicker of interest in the more general withdrawal. See for instance, the observation on page 51.

CHILDREN'S FEELINGS

Acceptable needs – unacceptable outlet

Adults coping with young children can easily get stuck with the behaviour that they find hard to handle and not consider what might be motivating a child. A good example is the behaviour that adults call 'attention-seeking'. Children's methods of getting attention can have a disruptive effect but it is perfectly reasonable that they should want attention; being 'attention seeking' is not in itself reprehensible. Children have emotional needs: to feel recognised, that they have an importance in their own social world, are liked, accepted and are competent. Difficulties arise from some of the ways that children learn to satisfy those needs or to cope with feelings of not being valued or noticed. Adults are responsible for recognising the underlying emotional needs and helping children to find less disruptive ways of coping.

Other ways to express the same feeling

Children have strong feelings, just like adults. They too feel anger, embarrassment, fear, distress, sadness, depression, excitement or the wish to retaliate. Sometimes the strength of their feelings can seem overwhelming to children. If their frustration has spilled over into a tantrum or into hurtful remarks to someone they love, children can be frightened by the power of their emotions and need reassurance that what they have done or said has not caused permanent harm.

Sometimes you need to reassure children that having strong feelings is normal, that everyone sometimes feels afraid or angry. It will not help a child to cope if the adult reaction is to deny or reject those feelings with comments like 'You're making a fuss about nothing' or 'Big boys don't cry'. More sensitive adults, and those whom the child will later trust, accept the feelings and see what they can do to help before a child reaches a high emotional pitch. You also need to see whether immediate comfort to a frustrated child will help to calm him down or whether you can – another time if not this time – guide a child towards expressing feelings through a different channel. For example, a child who gets very excited, described from the adult viewpoint as 'over-excited', can have this energy directed into active outdoor games. When it is appropriate for the child, he can be guided into calmer activities.

Some children may always have a short fuse on anger or else they may have learned to express annoyance loudly and physically from their family model. You need to take as the starting point that the angry feelings exist and then help a child to learn that, in your setting, you will not allow her to kick other people or scream abuse. You cannot expect to guide her towards total quiet or patience but perhaps she will learn to stamp her feet in irritation rather than kick another child. Perhaps she will say 'I'm cross with you!' rather than swear.

Talking together

Of course, if adults want children to express feelings through words or to tell you what is happening with another child rather than lash out physically, then you have to make time to listen and show you take children's emotions seriously. Give attention to help children to express feelings and learn the words to say how they feel. You might make encouraging comments like, 'Do you feel all cross about what just happened with Jason?' or 'You don't look very happy, Ayesha. Do you want to tell me about it?' If you are dealing with an unhappy child then you may have to give time and attention before the child trusts you and comes out of her shell. A seriously unhappy or depressed child may be hard to help in a busy group and in this situation you might need additional professional help.

Speaking up or telling tales
A trap for children who have been encouraged to speak up rather than lash out can be that they unwittingly cross the line into behaviour that adults call 'telling tales'. This area is an adult responsibility: it is important to be clear yourself on the boundary line and to be consistent in a staff group, including playgroup helpers in a school. It is not unusual that adults will say that 'coming to tell' is clearly different from 'telling tales' but the children often do not see the situation that way.

Undoubtedly you want children to feel able to cope with minor difficulties and you want to discourage children who wish to get another child into trouble. You can use encouraging remarks such as 'I think you can sort that out yourselves' or to a reporter on other children 'I'd rather wait until one of them comes to tell me.'

RULES AND REASONS

Explaining rules

There are occasions when children genuinely do not understand what is expected of them. The limits may be so clear and obvious to adults that they fail to appreciate that some children have not grasped what is wanted and why. In a group setting children have to adjust to rules that are normal routine to the workers but may seem very odd to a child. Perhaps one child is used to helping at home and cannot understand why the nursery cook is angry that she has gone into the kitchen. Another child may be allowed to draw in her books at home or has mistaken a playgroup book for a drawing one. Either child has made a mistake, not been deliberately naughty. Any rules need to be clear to children, expressed positively as often as possible and given with a sensible explanation.

Asking children 'Why?'

Sometimes you will want to understand why a child has behaved in a certain way. It is rarely useful to ask the straightforward 'Why did you do that?' since children tend to hear this as an accusation and mutter 'because', 'he started it' or say nothing at all. The lack of a rational explanation can leave adults perplexed or cross.

Think about how adults tend to react if asked 'Why?' they have done something mildly reprehensible. Often you do not know exactly why or, faced with the question, you know your explanation will not sound good enough. In a confrontation with another adult most people do not react very coherently to comments like 'Why are you driving so fast!' The answer tends to be a counter-attack of 'Don't nag me about my driving!'

The problem with 'Why' is that it often has a critical ring to it. Children sense that they have already been judged and they are not being asked a real question. With children, as with adults, a genuine question or request may open up communication rather than close it. 'What' questions tend to be less accusing: 'What were you trying to do?' or 'Tell me what happened between you and John.'

Being 'good' – being 'bad'

The words 'good' and 'bad' are adult shorthand for a wide range of children's behaviours and adults' feelings about those behaviours. No two adults will share identical views on what exactly constitutes 'good' and 'bad' behaviour. Even for individual adults there tends to be some inconsistency, depending on the stresses of the situation. So, the words themselves are not very helpful because they give limited information to children. The problems of being seen as a 'bad' child are covered on page 136. Some space is given here to the downside of being 'good'.

Adults use 'good' as a compliment: 'There's a good girl' or 'You've been very good today, so you can have some chocolate'. Sometimes the compliment has a twist, as in 'Why can't you be good like your brother?' But this demand is likely to confuse a child; of all the 'good' things her brother has done, what is it that the adult wants this time? Is it being quiet, answering without a sulky expression, not making such a mess? Comparing children is rarely helpful to their relationship. At best the two have to hold on to good relations despite the adult interference and at worst they can be divided by the adult judgements. Talking of 'goodness' is rarely informative to children about adult expectations. But, having made the pronouncement 'Be good, or else!' the adult may be convinced that fair warning has been given.

The 'If you're good . . .' trap

This phrase is rarely, if ever, used between adults and it is a sobering lesson to do precisely that. Say to a colleague 'If you're good, then I'll wash up the coffee cups' or promise a friend or partner 'So long as you're good today, I'll take you to the cinema this evening'. Apart from looking surprised, the other adult will probably ask, 'What do you mean "good"?' or 'So what exactly do I have to do then?' Similar phrases are no more clear to children, who may well guess what you want, or part of it, but have to play detective based on what you've wanted in the past.

It is far better to be direct with children. Instead of saying, 'That's a good girl', tell a child what has pleased you with 'Well done, you finished all your lunch' or 'Thank you for helping me tidy up'. Avoid any contrasts between children of 'Why can't you be like ...' and look for genuine opportunities for children to help each other. The 'If you're good ...' promises or threats are far better expressed as specific requests, for instance 'Please be patient. I must write this message before I forget. Then I can help you.' Allowance has to be made, of course, for the very limited ability of younger children to wait.

A CONSIDERATE APPROACH TO CHILDREN

The risks of seeing children as the problem

When adults find children hard to handle, there is a danger that the children will be viewed almost totally through the disliked behaviour. Parents or other carers then notice any examples of the irritating behaviour more than any positive moves by children. Adults tend to react quickly to the annoyance, failing to see the glimmer of other possibilities. This leads to a serious risk that the child will be seen entirely in negative terms. She will be described as a bad-tempered child rather than one who sometimes loses her temper. The occasions when she is patient will be dismissed by 'Why can't you be like that more often!'

Once adults see a child wholly through the behaviour they dislike, their treatment of the child can lead her to see herself in this way. Unhappiness and a sense of 'I'm wrong whatever I do' will reduce the motivation to try to behave differently. A child who has been labelled as 'naughty' learns through experience that limited efforts in the 'good' direction do not bring as much attention as the 'naughty' actions. A vicious circle becomes established and the labelling of this child can travel with her as a report or reputation when she moves to a different early years setting or to school.

Keep behaviour separate from personality

You can help to stop the build-up of child = 'bad' behaviour by avoiding any labels for children, positive or negative. Children are individuals, with varying interests and aptitudes and with variations in qualities like patience, willingness to be cooperative or curiosity. Once a child has been labelled negatively (as 'spiteful' or ' a poor eater') or positively (as 'considerate' or 'patient'), the implication is that this is an unchanging part of the child's personality. Adult feelings about the negative labels tend to be fairly hopeless and sometimes self-fulfilling prophecies are set in place.

Positive labels

Adults are usually more aware of the dangers of negative labels on children. But the children given positive labels do not necessarily benefit. A child who is told 'You are such a patient little girl' or who overhears 'Steve is always so helpful' may begin to feel valued only in so far as they show these qualities. They may worry about the feelings and inclinations that they have that do not fit the 'good' image and wonder if adults would still like them if they realised that sometimes they are cross or do not feel like being helpful. Adults unthinkingly suggest these doubts are true when they make comments like 'Now that's not like you, is it Steve? I can usually depend on you to help.' This adult judgement imposes 'I know you best' and denies the right of the child sometimes not to feel helpful.

It is not always easy for adults to separate children's behaviour from feelings about what they are like as individuals. Your reactions to children are, of course, influenced by what the children do. However, it is fairer to deal with behaviour as patterns in which there can be variety. Thank any child for helpful behaviour with a specific, 'I finished that in half the time with your help. Thank you.' Such an approach also gives children clear guidance about your reactions. Avoid making sweeping statements about children, whether positive ('You're such a helpful boy') or negative ('Wouldn't it be nice if you could be like that more often').

Negative labels

When you want to discourage particular actions, it will be far more constructive for you to describe the behaviour that concerns you than to assign a label to a child. Think of a child as one who has firm ideas about what she wants to do and little patience in being offered alternatives. This firmness may stand her in good stead in other circumstances but is hard going in the playgroup. Such a description can give you more sense of room to work with the child than a blunt 'she's stubborn'.

It is possible, and helpful to children, to make a clear difference between actions and the individual. You try to view the situation as one in which you are frustrated or annoyed with a child but you are not dismissing her as an individual, you still value her. It is important to say this to children with comments such as 'Jon, I like you; I don't like your swearing.' Your other words and body language show also the message of 'We have to find a way to stop the swearing'. You can show children that you care about them and you will still be trying to guide them away from certain kinds of behaviour and towards alternatives. All children will misbehave in adults' eyes, many times, but they deserve the constant reassurance that their value does not waiver depending on what they have done. Never use comments like 'I won't like you if . . .' or 'I don't love you anymore because . . .'. Such remarks are cruel and undermine children's sense of self-worth. They also give a poor example for children to copy in their relationships.

A BALANCE BETWEEN POSITIVES AND NEGATIVES

'Do's and 'don't's

When you are working with a child or a group who are draining your energy, it is very easy to fall into a habit of stopping children rather than re-directing them. There seems to be no time to acknowledge when the children are managing well or helping each other. An onlooker or a tactful colleague may see the imbalance, or you may well realise that too many of the exchanges with children have become negative.

An imbalance towards 'don't' creates a miserable and dissatisfying atmosphere for children and adults alike. You feel that time with the children consists of annoyance and interruptions with little enjoyment. The children feel that you are no longer much fun to be with and why bother to behave well when there is so much nagging? The risk also develops that children learn that only disruptive behaviour successfully gets your attention.

This vicious circle has to be broken deliberately and by an adult:

- Consciously reduce your 'don't's. Be ready to stop them emerging from your mouth.
- Take some time to think over, perhaps discuss with a colleague, what is happening in your group (or in your home as a parent). What behaviour really must be stopped? What could be ignored because it is only at a low, niggling level?
- Think just as hard about how you would like the children to behave. About what actions can you be openly pleased?
- Increase your 'do's. Try hard that instead of using 'don't do that' you offer 'how about we . . .' or 'Let's sort this out . . .'
- Offer children a choice in terms of behaviour. This can be a positive strategy when you are becoming frustrated with repeating 'No' and 'Don't'.

For example:

The staff of Rhiannon Nursery School believe that local trips are an important part of the nursery curriculum and they like every child to have this opportunity. But Olwen has experienced several hair-raising incidents with four-year-old Damian who dashes off without warning on the street or in the market. Careful conversations with Damian have led to heartfelt promises to stay with the group that he has not been able to keep. Olwen does not want to ban Damian from the trips and discusses possible alternatives with Amy, the nursery head. Olwen then explained to Damian's mother what she would like to do, so that there would be no misunderstandings. In a friendly way, absolutely not as a punishment, Olwen will give Damian the choice of 'holding my hand like a big boy' or 'having the reins on like a little boy'. Walking freely and running off at will is not a choice on offer.

Each time that Olwen's group went out on a local trip, Damian was offered his choice. If he chose to hold Olwen's hand then he had to behave like a big boy and keep hold. Olwen took the opportunity to encourage Damian with comments such as 'It's nice to walk together; I can talk with you easier.' If Damian chose the reins then Olwen made no negative comments and she discouraged any remarks from the other children like 'Damian's a baby!' Olwen's explanation to the others was that 'Damian's having a tough time getting used to how to behave on trips. But he'll get there in the end.'

Over five or six trips Damian became bored with the reins choice, agreed to hold a hand and kept the promise. Within several weeks Olwen felt confident enough to let go and Damian stayed within a few metres of the group.

Giving choices

The kind of choice described in the boxed example can be offered to younger children but with the emphasis on actions and not words. A young child who finds she is taken away from the play when she pinches other children will learn in time not to pinch, so long as she is not distracted from this message by adult irritation. Choices can be used at home as well as in a group. Children who are refusing an evening bath can be given the choice of 'Would you like to walk yourself or shall I carry you to the bathroom?' The possibility of escaping the bath is not offered.

So long as giving choices in not over-used it can be a constructive way to focus both child and adult on what can happen rather than on what is forbidden or a source of argument. The approach can help children because it gives them a feeling of some control over events. The offer of choice is ruined if there are any overtones of punishment.

Encouraging children seen as difficult

It is so easy for your attention to be drawn to children mainly when you feel they are being a nuisance. So it is important to know what they are doing when they are not being experienced as a problem by you. Children might be absorbed in activities that you could join or open to being helped by you. It happens all too often that adults heave a sigh of relief when a child they find difficult is out of sight and quiet.

To encourage more positive behaviour, you need to be clear in your own mind about what you would like children to do, rather than concentrating your energies on what you want them to stop doing. Try this as a constructive exercise:

1 Write down a clear description of what an individual child does that you find irritating or disruptive.

2 Then against each negative description, write a specific example of how you would like the child to behave in that situation. The example must be phrased positively, so no sentences beginning, 'She'll stop . . .'

You may not find this shift to the positive an easy exercise but it is worth your time. When life has become very fraught with a child then a focused observation (for instance see page 49) may also support your efforts. If you work to envisage the positive alternatives you gain two advantages:

- You may realise that the child does behave in this way sometimes and you are not acknowledging those times.
- You have a direction in which to encourage a child and a clearer vision.

The drawbacks of punishment

Punishment is not generally an effective way of helping anyone to learn. Physical punishment of children, through hitting or shaking, is an abusive use of adults' greater strength and power and is unacceptable in any early years setting. Yet spoken recriminations and a range of looks and gestures can say just as clearly say 'What a hopeless effort' or 'Stupid child!' in a discouraging and negative way.

Used as a way of controlling children's behaviour, punishment gives only the negative information of 'Don't do that'. It does not say clearly 'I want you to do this instead'. Children on the receiving end of punishment often feel confused, guessing about what the adult wants or losing sight of their behaviour altogether because of the upset or anger about the punishment. Adults can be blinkered over the child's perspective, claiming 'Of course, she knows what she should be doing' or 'I have to punish her, how else will she learn?'

The effects of punishment are unpredictable. Children who wish to please or who are cowed by the punishment, will stop doing what was punished but new ways of coping will not emerge. Children who like drama and confrontation may increase the behaviour in enjoyable defiance. Spoken, unspoken or physical punishment also blocks learning because of the feelings aroused. Children who are punished may feel anxious, humiliated, confused, angry or vengeful; none of these emotions will support efforts to behave differently.

Punishment is often satisfying to the adult giving it. Shouting at a child expresses frustrations and annoyances. It is a way of letting off steam, perhaps for paying a child back for 'showing me up in front of everybody'. Anger is also sometimes the adult response to their own fear that children have put themselves in danger. How many times have you seen a parent pull a child back from running into the road only then to shout at or even hit the child? The safety lesson is lost in the punishment.

Caring for and raising children is a task with as many frustrations as pleasures and adults will make mistakes. It would be unrealistic to say you must never say a cross word to a child. But it is important to realise that this type of punishment is of little value other than making you feel better. You often do not even give children a clear idea of your feelings, for instance when fear emerges as anger.

When you need to speak or act firmly with a child, then it is best to be brief and close in time to the child's behaviour. If it seems most appropriate to take a child away from her play, or a toy away from her, then act immediately on the incident and the removal should not last long. For under-twos, especially, the point can be made in the few moments it takes to hold them steady, look directly at the child and say 'No. No biting.' Even older children are best dealt with by reprimands and sanctions that last no more than a few minutes. Otherwise resentment and confusion can set in.

With four- and five-year-olds, it can be possible to use some future sanction as a punishment, since they will remember over a longer period, but this still has drawbacks. Suppose a four-year-old hit the baby an a hour ago. He is now told 'I said if you hit the baby, you couldn't help me at teatime'. The child probably recalls the incident but since then has probably been reasonably well-behaved. Yet the baby-hitting incident is being held against him into the future and has lost him a privilege that is not linked logically with the baby. Ideally, it is better to deal with incidents as they occur and then to continue with a clean sheet.

If you are in a nursery or playgroup it is unwise to hold threats over children of 'I'll tell your parents what you did'. Firstly, parents may not be at all pleased to be used as a threat in this way. Secondly, you should deal with most incidents within the group. Some situations may require that you communicate with parents: a serious difficulty, one which you are working with the parents to improve or an incident which has left marks. You can still avoid a threatening approach by telling a child 'I will have to talk to your Mum when she comes. But I'll let you say your bit as well.'

Using consequences

The most effective use of less pleasant events for children is for adults to be calmly consistent about certain consequences following from certain actions of the child. There are two different ways of using consequences.

Natural consequences
A child can experience the inevitable natural consequences of her actions. If she leaves her books out in the rain then they will get wet and possibly spoil. If she does not eat her lunch then she will probably be hungry before teatime. The experienced pressure of reality can be an effective way for children to learn that their choices have consequences that they may not enjoy. Children are, of course, denied this opportunity if a parent nags about the books and gets them in when the child does nothing, or if children are allowed to snack between lunch and tea. There are, of course, some natural

consequences that no responsible adult would allow a child to risk, such as the likely results of dashing out into a busy road.

Logical consequences
This type of consequence is determined by an adult, for example, removing toys that a child is mis-using. If logical consequences are to work, you have to:

- Warn children about what will happen if they continue.
- Follow through calmly if they do continue.

For instance, a child is not allowed to rip the pages of her books. If she starts to tear, she is warned with 'No, Sandra, you don't rip the books. I'll take them away . . .' If Sandra continues to rip then the books are taken and you offer some other activity. If later she asks for her books once more, she can be trusted but the books are removed promptly if she starts tearing again. An older child can be given the explanation calmly: 'When you're ready to look at the book and not tear the pages, you can have it back.'

A young child can understand simple words and body language that give the same message: a firm 'No', head-shaking and removal of the toy or book. There are also practical steps to take with young children, such as not leaving them unsupervised with play materials that they may mis-use.

Learning without nagging
Use of consequences can help children to learn so long as adults resist the temptation to nag or hark back once an incident is over. The child starts afresh each time as snide remarks or recriminations will disrupt the learning.

Perhaps a child has her bike temporarily removed by her father because she insists on riding it into the family cat. The father has told the child twice to be careful of the cat but nothing has changed and the bike is removed. Later on the child is looking wistfully at her bike and her father offers 'Are you ready to ride the bike carefully now?' If the child agrees then she has the bike but if she rides it over the cat then the bike is promptly removed. The child is given a chance to show she can be trusted and to make a choice. But she does not have a completely free choice; if she chooses to ram the cat, then this means no more bike. As children get older, it becomes more possible to have a conversation with them about limits and consideration for others. Younger children may not understand what you are saying (see for instance page 120 on the feelings of others).

Adult behaviour
A number of strategies that adults use in punishing ways are better applied as consequences. The difference is created through your own adult behaviour. For many years one of the ways that adults have dealt with unacceptable behaviour has been by removing children: putting them in corners, on 'naughty chairs' or outside the room. If this is done with adult anger, perhaps when you snap at the last straw, then it operates as a

punishment, especially since children then tend to be left for an indeterminate length of time until the adults calms down. When the actions happen in a flurry of adult irritation, children often also have to deal with gibes from other children.

A calm-down period can work effectively as a consequence and the organised use of this strategy is called 'time out'. This approach will work so long as:

- Removal of a child follows consistently from specific behaviours. The strategy is not used for a long list of actions.
- Children are given a calm warning and a chance to behave.
- The removal is calm and the child stays only a few minutes, maximum, in the calm-down place.
- The child can return after calming down with no nagging from the adult and prevention of any teasing or jibes from other children.

The aim of this pattern is that children become progressively more able to guide their own behaviour. When they cannot stop themselves the removal is viewed as a 'fair cop'. This strategy can also work in the family home, so long as the above guidelines are followed.

ENCOURAGEMENT AND REWARDS

The value of encouragement and how it differs from reward are discussed on page 60. Many of the practical suggestions offered throughout this book depend on encouraging children's efforts at least as often as praising their achievements. In this chapter there has been a focus on encouraging children towards how you would like them to behave or towards one method of coping with stress rather than another. The focus on encouragement is not meant to suggest that reward should never be used. Rewards, used sparingly and in a specific approach, can be effective in helping children to change some behaviour.

One method of helping older children to deal with wetting or soiling accidents is to build in simple rewards for success but avoid punishment for failure. The reward might be immediate and tangible, such as ten pence for every dry night. Alternatively, the reward might be a star to stick on a chart, when the understanding is that a certain number of stars can be traded for a special treat. Children younger than four or five years are not likely to understand the symbols of a star chart and so this method is not appropriate.

The emphasis of stars or similar systems is that success is celebrated. No stars or ticks are taken away for failure and you need to explain this carefully if you are working with parents on such a system. Eventually, of course, you want a child to behave well or manage dry pants for personal satisfaction. So there needs to be a steady progression from a reward for every success to reward to a certain numbers of successes and then to an end to the system. Encouragement needs to be regular so that children do not feel that their behaviour no longer matters.

The risk of over-using rewards for behaviour is that adults can set a trap for themselves which children gleefully exploit. Certain kinds of behaviour, such as helping with the tidying up, are expected because that makes life run more smoothly and is part of the adult vision of how you are helping children to learn. Unpleasant experiences, such as taking a dose of medicine, have to be managed and it is unwise to get into the cul-de-sac that lets a child say 'You gave me twenty pence last time I took this horrid medicine. I want twenty pence now.' It is a less hazardous course to be supportive of the child, to help them to get the medicine down and then to say 'Well done' for having managed something unpleasant but necessary. Special outings or treats are given because they are fun and enjoyable, not as variable events depending on whether children are 'good'.

THE FOCUS ON ADULTS

All adults spending time with children – as workers or parents – need to recognise their own contribution to any situation. It is far too easy, especially if you feel under pressure, to focus on what the children are doing and how you feel they ought to change. But, adults are the ones with more experience and a broader perspective, not to mention what should be a more mature level of development! How we behave makes a difference to children and a focus on adults is a recognition of this fact – not a shifting of blame. Adults can make a positive difference to children through setting a good example for children to follow, being prepared to find a way out of difficult encounters that a child could not be expected to see and by constantly looking to boost children's sense of self-worth and not undermine it.

9

RESPONDING POSITIVELY TO HOW CHILDREN BEHAVE

A child alone does not make a problem; somebody has to experience her as a problem. Because adults vary, their judgements will differ over whether they find a child hard to handle or whether she is more difficult to deal with than another child. Some adults find particular types of behaviour hard to tolerate. Perhaps they can remain calm while a child makes hurtful remarks but lose that calmness if a child spits at them. Not all potential problems with children are noticed equally quickly. In a group such as a playgroup or nursery, the noisy problems of aggression or destructiveness may seem very obvious. Yet the distress of a depressed child or lack of interest of a very withdrawn child may go unnoticed for some time, especially by less experienced workers.

PHYSICAL AGGRESSION

Different types

Most young children act aggressively at some time. Their lives are full of frustrations which may seem minor to adults but can become all-absorbing to children. A physical reaction can seem the most satisfactory solution, especially if children have limited ability to express themselves in words.

There is a wide variation in how children express physical aggression:

- A child may be indiscriminately aggressive, lashing out at anyone who is close at hand – people or pets.
- Some children may attack those younger or smaller than themselves, including babies. Perhaps they sense the power of being larger and the limited risk of being attacked in return. For a harassed younger child in a large family, the younger children in nursery may be the first opportunity to unload feelings onto someone smaller.
- Some children turn their aggression against specific adults.

Physical aggression is a problem that tends to bring adults running. In some cases the sheer noise of the confrontation brings attention. Alternatively, children who are sly in their pinching or hitting may outrage adults because of the sneaky nature of the attack. Aggression is a problem hard to ignore, although different standards may be applied by different adults and some certainly tolerate higher levels of aggressive behaviour from boys than girls.

Many of the situations covered in this chapter will benefit from the observation techniques described in Part 1. Labelling a child as 'aggressive' says very little about what the child does and is no firm basis for working out a positive approach. Observation can help you to understand any patterns and the level of seriousness: whom the child attacks, under what circumstances and how often genuinely unprovoked attacks happen. So please consider this chapter together with Part 1, especially Chapter 3.

Stepping in before the aggression

There are times when children can deal with a situation themselves and, if you keep an eye on events, they can learn safely that they do not always need an adult referee. Sometimes experience will tell you that you cannot let events unfold without somebody getting hurt.

When you judge that intervention is wise, you may simply step in to resolve a dispute, split up children or guide one child away from the action before tempers fray beyond repair. Sometimes, you may be able to distract the child who tends towards aggression into some other activity, more attention from you and maybe an energetic activity to release some of the tensions. Unfortunately there will be times when a child is unwilling to be diverted or a physical attack is clearly imminent – the hand is drawn back or this child's face tells you that she is just about to bite. In these circumstances, you can physically prevent a child by catching her hand or holding back her entire body so she cannot bite. You can reinforce your preventative action with a firm 'No'. If you are on the other side of the room, a shout of 'Liam! No!' may halt a child who has learned from previous occasions that you do not allow aggression. You would then need to move swiftly to the child's side.

After an aggressive attack

Sometimes, in a busy group or the family home, you will not be able to get there in time. Your aim is then to act after the event so as to bring home the lesson that aggressive behaviour is not acceptable. A sharp word to the aggressor and plenty of affectionate attention to the child on the receiving end can show the former that she or he loses out through such unpleasantness. Children can be requested to apologise to children they have hurt but there is little point in insisting. Some children simply learn the formula of 'Sorry, sorry' in order to escape from the unwelcome adult attention. (See also page 120 on helping children to develop empathy.)

It is very important, of course, that children who have to be reprimanded for aggressive behaviour still gain plenty of attention and encouragement when they are not being aggressive.

Example: Explaining strategies to parents

Boundaries Playgroup has a difficult situation with children whose parents have told them to hit or bite back. There was an especially unpleasant incident when one mother came into the playgroup and threatened a child whom she claimed had bitten her son with 'I'll bite you! Then you'll know how it feels!'

After discussion with the team, Marion, the playgroup leader, called a general parents' meeting on positive approaches to behaviour in the playgroup and put together a simple leaflet to hand out. The main points on this specific issue were:

- We do not encourage children to hit or bite back because that muddles our message that we do not want any hitting or biting at all. Please help us – don't tell your child it is all right to hit back.
- Young children who are told it is fine to hit back tend to use this permission in situations when they have not been hit but are just in an argument with another child.
- We never retaliate against a child with the same aggressive behaviour because this would set such a bad example to them. We would effectively be saying 'Never mind what I do! Just do what I tell you!'
- Please think very carefully when you are tempted to hit your children back or bite them. What will you do if this does not work first time? Hit them harder? Give two bites in return for every single one? This can get dangerously out of hand.

And in the discussion the playgroup team described the different strategies they used in the group.

Consistent behaviour from adults

You can choose to take a child who has been aggressive into a quiet area to calm down. The strategy of 'time out' (see also page 142) can be an effective way of marking the incident and expressing your disapproval. Younger children, under-threes, are unlikely to understand the link between what they have done and time out. It can be better to hold a child to face you and say a firm 'No hitting' or 'Absolutely no biting'. Sometimes it will be necessary for you to take a break from the child so that you can calm down.

Ideally, you need to make your point every time that a child behaves aggressively, deal with the incident swiftly and move on. Lengthy explanations or recriminations are rarely effective. Even if they could understand the ideas you are communicating, children who are being told off stop listening after a while.

If an appropriate consequence of aggression is to remove play materials from a child or the child from an activity, then your action should be as immediate and calm as you can manage. Adult reactions should never drag on through the day since a constructive use of consequences then becomes a punishment (see also page 139). Children will swiftly forget the original reason and focus only on what is happening now – that they are being stopped from doing favourite activities or that other children are being allowed to treat them as a 'naughty child'.

Talking with parents
Sometimes it will make sense to speak with a parent at the end of the day about a child's behaviour – aggressive actions or some of the other difficulties covered in this chapter. A good working relationship with parents means that you will need sometimes to have potentially difficult conversations about children's behaviour. A few private words can bring a parent up to date with what happened, how you handled the situation and perhaps how the child made amends. Long-running difficulties may need an appointment with a parent for a lengthier conversation. (See also page 193.)

AGGRESSION EXPRESSED IN WORDS

Aggressive feelings are not always expressed through physical attacks, difficulties can also arise from what is said. Some children have learned to shout abuse, taunt other children or to swear.

Dealing with insults

You may feel hurt by what children say to you but it is better not to rise to a child's verbal attack. Try hard to deal with the emotion underlying the child's words. There is an element of guesswork in judging what could lead a child to make hurtful remarks to you or to another child.

- Sometimes the child may feel she is replying fairly in kind to another child who has hurt her, or that you have really hurt her feelings without realising. Such incidents are best handled by ignoring the words used and dealing with what led to them.
- Some children wish to hurt others as they have been hurt themselves, outside your immediate setting.
- Some enjoy the power of upsetting other children and adults but sometimes children make vicious-sounding remarks, like 'I wish you were dead' or 'I hate you' because in their anger or distress they do not know a milder way of expressing their feelings.

Not rising to insult
There is scope for ignoring the remarks of a child who has made a habit of mildly insulting other people. If other children learn not to rise to the insult then the child may feel there is little point in continuing. Younger children, certainly those under four

or five years, can find ignoring the insults hard and need adult support. You probably need to allow some leeway to children in your setting for answering back. You may say there is to be no hitting in retaliation but it is really not fair to ban any form of verbal reply. It depends of course on what children are saying to each other. You should not let some remarks pass.

Stepping in to challenge some remarks

There are some types of insult that should not be ignored: offensive remarks that criticise a child's culture or ethnic group, insults to a child based on gender or that call negative attention to a disability. What you say will depend on the words and you need to leave space for the child to listen and understand. On one occasion, your best approach might be 'That's not a word I want you to use in our nursery. It is very rude towards children like Dorcas who are black.' Another time you might gently challenge a remark with 'That's not true, you know. Boys can do needlework and Alex can join us. What made you think only girls do needlework?' On yet another time a positive approach might be more 'I believe that you hurt Lynne's feelings by saying what you did about her hand.'

Whatever the type of remark, you need to encourage children who insult others to shift their behaviour. A child who regularly makes very hurtful comments needs to be told firmly 'I like you Darren; I don't like it when you say . . .' A long-term approach would be to support the child in feeling powerful through other means or to try to help with the child's own hurt which is expressed through retaliation. Time spent with children will give you clues to the feelings that lie below the surface. Children can discover that they are liked, in fact you have persisted in liking them despite what they said. Alternatively you may give children experience of responsibility or a role in the group that gives a sense of special identity without having to put down the other children.

Swearing

Children swear for a number of different reasons and your approach has to fit with what you judge is happening with this particular child.

Some children undoubtedly swear in complete innocence. They have heard the words – in the family, on the street or from television – and these are just new words. In these circumstances, it is often effective to tell children that this is a rude word or unpleasant phrase and you do not want to hear it at the nursery. When children bring in words they hear at home you may also need to talk with the parent(s) and explain your actions for nursery. A child whose family swears a great deal may genuinely not know the difference between words which are swearing and those which are not.

Some children may not know the meaning of swear words but they appreciate that they are 'naughty' words that have the power to shock. When children are trying to create an effect it is better to show no upset or shock. Ignoring the child may work in a small group since, without a reaction, the child may not bother to try to shock you again. However, ignoring is not usually a workable approach because:

- Children often persevere and step up the swearing so that you have to respond.
- If you do not allow the swear words, or racist phrases, in the group then you should say this the first time. Apart from being consistent with your rules, the child who has made a mistake needs to know.
- Other children will probably not let the incident go and take the line that 'You're not allowed to say that here!'

Your best approach is to register the swearing, with a calm comment that the word is not to be said here or with a firmer 'That's enough!', depending on how the child is behaving. Avoid a tirade against the child and play down any drama from the other children with 'Yes, I heard what Danny said and I've told him not to.' You may also need to ensure that other adults do not add to the potential drama with 'Did you hear what he said!', since this is embarrassing to the child who has made a mistake and provides an audience for the child who has set out to shock.

Children need to express their emotions and so it can help to provide children with alternative words or phrases to be said with feeling in times of frustration of hurt. These have to be words that you use naturally, perhaps 'Sugar!' or 'Rats!'. Children who use swear words for emphasis, probably following the example of a parent or character on television, can be guided towards alternatives in lively expression. For instance, you might repeat a sentence in which you have replaced a word: 'Look at that bloody big dog' becomes 'Yes, look at that e-nor-mous dog' when you give dramatic emphasis to the new word.

DESTRUCTIVENESS

Some children are destructive towards things rather than aggressive towards people; some show both types of behaviour. Children who turn their feelings onto objects may tear up books, empty packages of food at home or throw toys around. Some develop dangerous patterns of behaviour such as fire-raising.

Most of the points suggested about aggression are also appropriate to destructive behaviour.

- Try to step in to prevent an outburst if knowledge of the child suggests that this is likely.
- Firm but brief words or physically restraining her are better than shouting matches or flurries of adult activity.

- After the child has been destructive, brief expressions of adult disapproval are better than lengthy tirades.
- Offer children the opportunity to clear up any mess they have made and make it clear that 'I would like you to help me in putting this right.' The time may come when the child will respond to an approach that implies 'You're big enough to make this mess, so I'm sure you're capable of clearing it up.' Clearing up is not a punishment; the child is accepting some responsibility for the consequences of her actions. Children should be thanked if they do clear up or make a genuine apology to a child they have hurt.
- Children may refuse or only clear up half-heartedly and it is doubtful whether full-scale arguments over the issue will help. Consider what logical or natural consequences you might impose (see page 140) and make sure that you are consistent with your colleagues.
- Adults are responsible for taking sensible measures to avoid children's doing harm to themselves or others. In a family home, for instance, parents should move matches to a secure place, keep sharp implements out of children's reach and supervise children properly.

Adults' feelings and reactions

Children's age is relevant in making sense of this problem. Very young children who have learned the physical skills of throwing may well throw objects indiscriminately and have no idea that they will break or hurt people. Children have to learn that some things are not for throwing and that balls bounce but china plates smash. Likewise, they have to learn that, although it may be allowed to rip up old magazines, books have to be treated differently.

Drama can be associated with children who behave destructively and it is important that adults remain as calm as possible and not retaliate with anger. Calmness is hard to maintain when a child is throwing things at you or has hurt other children. But if a child's behaviour is fired partly by a wish for attention and a sense of powerfulness, then signs of panic or strong emotions from adults may only encourage the behaviour.

Calmness is important at the time but you need to acknowledge your own feelings and have a chance to talk about the situation. A physically strong four- or five-year-old can be frightening. It is possible that she or he could hurt you and the unpredictability of some children can make you feel that you are sitting on a small volcano. In a group, adults need to support one another in dealing with the feelings and, despite the unease or anxiety, help one another to hold on to a consistent approach to the destructive outbursts.

In calmer moments
As hard as it can be, you need to treat a child given to destructive behaviour in as nor-

mal a way as possible. There is a real risk that children may be hedged around with many prohibitions in order to guard against outbursts. You should be alert to a child's warning signs and, in a family home, should make sure that you are especially cautious about household safety. But, other than simple caution, further restrictions of a child are more likely to raise frustration. Children may need to learn that there are other ways of exercising power and gaining an audience. Perhaps they can demonstrate a skill in front of the other children, or make them laugh rather than run for cover. With care, children may react well to being given simple responsibilities including taking care of equipment.

Reducing the drama

It is easy to be drawn into the 'excitement' around children who pose the noisier problems — aggression, destructiveness or tantrums. Even experienced adults can become absorbed in the awful aspects of a child rather than positive sides. A child may become a topic of conversation — 'You'll never guess what Billy did today' — or fuel for exchanges such as 'My group are far more of a handful than yours'. Although understandable, this outlook will not lead to a positive approach to the child. The unhelpful drama can sometimes be seen more easily by an onlooker and adults have to help one another, with tact, to see how far they may have become enmeshed in the drama and possibly made matters worse.

This is an important, though difficult, point to communicate when you are helping a parent. Certainly, some parents seem unwilling to make changes at home such as supervising a child more closely or removing matches or other dangerous household objects, whilst wanting professionals to sympathise with them over the awfulness of their child's behaviour.

TEMPER TANTRUMS

It is not unusual for the rising twos and two-year-olds to become angry and emotionally distressed. A wide range of events can tip children into minor or major temper tantrums: from being unable to make a toy work to being refused an ice cream, from a change in the usual routine to the end of a special treat. As children grow older, adults' efforts to be patient pay off and the children become more amenable to reason or to being offered alternatives. They can more easily understand explanations from adults and prior warnings such as 'We're going home after this cartoon has finished.'

Some older children still have many tantrums as a reaction to the continuing frustration in their lives (see, for instance the case study on page 14). There can be different reasons why some children do not grow out of the tantrums more usual for younger ones:

- Perhaps when the children were younger, adults gave in to their wishes at the first sign of temper.
- The lives of some children are so confusing and unpredictable that tantrums are more an expression of distress and lack of control than temper as such.
- The key adults in a child's life may fly into a rage at the slightest provocation, so the child has never learned any other way of dealing with disagreements or minor frustrations.

Handling the tantrum of a young child needs patience and a willingness to see the world from the child's standpoint. A parent might need to acknowledge that a child has been patient in four shops, so is it really crucial to carry on into a fifth and sixth? Parents and other carers need to be willing to say 'Sorry' with words and a cuddle when the realisation dawns that you have fought over an issue which was not really important. You also need to be honest with yourself how far your feelings of pride or embarrassment affected how you handled a situation.

Relative size can be a major difference in dealing with tantrums from a two or a four-year-old. You will most likely be able to lift the younger children and remove them, if necessary. On the other hand, lifting a struggling four-year-old is the way that some early years workers damage their backs. If possible, deal with the older children on the spot, comforting or physically keeping them safe as appropriate. A positive difference between the ages is that the older children may be more able to talk about an incident later, so long as you show sensitivity to their feelings. More general points apply across the age range.

Trying to avoid tantrums

It is sometimes possible to see a tantrum building up and, with knowledge of individual children, you may be able to distract children, comfort them or jolly them out of bad humour. Sometimes you may judge your best approach is to leave the immediate situation; some children calm down without an audience. Another child, you may know from experience, can be calmed by a chance to express anger in words.

Some tantrums build up as children sense that an adult is undecided, for instance whether the child can have sweets or some treat. Uncertain limits and inconsistency from adults tend to encourage children to try their luck – perhaps with a tantrum. Wavering between 'Yes' and 'No' , and being seen to waver by the child, provides an opportunity to influence the decision by throwing a tantrum, especially in a public place. Children are far less likely to try this tactic if experience tells them that 'No' does not mean 'Maybe'. A sensible parent or carer still gives time to reflect on whether they are fighting battles that are not very important. It is possible to be drawn into a confrontation mainly on the grounds of 'He's got to learn who's boss!'

Dealing with a child in a tantrum

Once children have gone into a tantrum they are beyond reason – even a child who will usually listen calmly to explanations. Calming words from an adult may slowly have an effect but it will be the emotional tone of what you say that calms rather than the actual words. Some children may be able to shout and kick out their anger in a corner without being restrained and it is unwise to start an unnecessary physical struggle with a child. Other children need to be safely contained and in some cases physically prevented from hurting themselves or others. As they emerge from the tantrum, children often need comfort, especially if the fierceness of their emotions has frightened them. An older child may be able and want to put some feelings into words or listen to an explanation from an adult.

You can help the situation – before, during and after – by remaining as calm as possible, doing what needs to be done to keep the child safe and not answering anger with further anger, which will only add to the drama and complicate the calm-down afterwards.

Children who throw fierce tantrums may need to be removed to a quiet part of the room, where they cannot hurt others. You need to think carefully about removal of the child from the room itself. This approach will not help if the consequence is that the child gets the full attention of another adult, perhaps in the centre office. Children will learn to throw tantrums to gain what they see as special attention, just as they will if they have learned that adults cave in swiftly to children's anger.

DEFIANCE AND LACK OF COOPERATION

Behaviour which adults call 'defiant' tends to cover a wide range of actions. Perhaps children flatly refuse to eat certain foods, or they are always the one to take out the special books without asking, or maybe they cannot resist having the last word in an argument. You may well have observed that different adults vary in their tolerance of any questioning or disagreement from children.

There can be many reasons underlying behaviour that seems uncooperative.

- Some children may enjoy defying an adult and then watching the reaction.
- The family experience of some children is that the only way to get an adult's undivided attention is to provoke a confrontation.
- A form of uncooperativeness that infuriates some adults is when children are very slow in all they do and the adult is convinced that the child could go faster. Some children are genuinely uncertain in what they are doing, some appear to want the attention of an adult who moves in to help.

A constructive approach

How many instructions?

A child who is seen as being 'uncooperative' is often given more instructions than other children, since adults assume, without probably being aware, that this child will not react without a great deal of persuasion. A child who has come to be seen as the 'naughty' one of the group is often chided for actions that would be ignored from other children. Banging her spoon on the table is yet another example of how irritating this child is and how she will not behave reasonably even for a moment. Spoon banging from another child might be seen as excitement over the coming meal or simple pleasure in making a rhythmic sound pattern.

It is important to monitor yourself if you are working with a child whom you feel will not cooperate — or you are a parent frustrated with your own child.

- Consciously reduce the number of instructions you give to the child and give her a chance to follow what you ask before repeating yourself.
- Make sure that you have the child's attention by being close to her and using her name.
- Sometimes it makes sense with older children to ask them to repeat back what you have asked in their own words – 'So tell me, Angie, what are you going to do next?'
- Encourage him to follow an instruction by making the time to accompany him through the movements or towards the place he is supposed to go. For example, you tidy up with the child or walk him to another play activity and away from the play that he is disrupting.

Positive compromises

You can often meet a child halfway and a compromise that you choose to offer is a strong option, not a sign of weakness. Discuss with other adults, who deal with the same child, ways that you all might ignore smaller issues and save any potential confrontation for times when the child must cooperate with what you ask. You might, for instance, agree that you will all ignore drumming of feet beneath the dinner table (or will deal with very noisy drumming in a calm way) but that the child must conform to the centre rule that bikes are not to ridden through the part of the garden used by the very young children.

Children who are slow

Some adults become very irritated when children take ages over everyday activities such as dressing or eating a meal. They take over with a 'Come on, slowcoach, I'll do it'. A child who has little motivation to try is then encouraged to act in a helpless way and a child who has genuine difficulty in the task is not helped to learn. Children with learning difficulties or physical disabilities may have genuine problems in managing a task. Other children may well need help and persistent encouragement. Perhaps you can divide up a task, such as dressing, so that the child completes part and you also help. If children receive a genuine, 'Well done' for what they have managed, they may be encouraged to take on a little more next time.

Example:

In Kingfisher Family Centre, the team have had many discussions about Andy's behaviour. His mother takes the view that Andy, who is nearly four years old, is out of her control and his father thinks that it is all the mother's fault for being soft on the boy. Gareth and Pippa, who work most with the family, have been following a pattern to defuse the power struggles that were becoming a daily event:

- Clear ground rules for those times that Andy must do what he is asked. A conscious effort to ignore backchat and argument from Andy.
- Acceptance that Andy responds better to Gareth. Pippa also deals with Andy but Gareth takes the lead in working to shift the child's behaviour.
- A deliberate effort to give Andy some specific responsibilities within the group and to ask his opinion. Andy has reacted well to working with Gareth and a second child on the reorganisation of the home corner.
- Gareth and Pippa are having several sessions with Andy's parents who are sceptical but willing at least to talk about different ways of handling their son's behaviour.

Lack of cooperation over meals

Refusals to eat, or to drink, can become an issue for workers responsible for a group of children. You may worry that other children will also refuse to eat. This does not seem to happen often but messy behaviour at mealtimes, such as flicking food, can spread if the first perpetrators are not reprimanded.

Several practical issues can arise:

- Mealtimes can be more social and it is easier to pace the eating if workers are taking their meal with the children at the same time.
- Children may join a nursery or full-day playgroup with little or no experience of sitting down to meals with others. Some families live largely on take-away food or eat off laps in front of the television. You are helping these children to learn a new way of behaving and patience is required.
- Children have food preferences as much as adults. It is not fair to expect them to like and eat up everything. It should go without saying that children should never be pushed to eat food that is contrary to their family's diet – whether that preference is for religious or other reasons.
- In a diverse area with different ethnic groups, children will bring a variety of meal-time habits to your setting. In some cultures, it is good manners to eat with fingers,

or with a range of different cutlery. Even cultures that routinely use a knife and fork do not all wield them in an identical way. Your mealtimes should show respect for different ways and you can help a child learn alternative ways of dealing with food without implying that their family ways are wrong.

Smaller appetites

Children who do not eat much are better given a smaller helping they will finish than a larger helping that they have to be nagged to eat. You can then be encouraging that a child has enjoyed the meal or been willing to try a portion of something new. Allowing children to serve themselves from larger dishes can make it more likely that they finish the meal they have chosen for quantity and balance. This approach obviously needs your supervision but the element of choice can defuse mealtimes that are becoming a battleground.

Example: personal observation

I have sat at many meal tables in nurseries and all-day playgroups. I have seen considerably fewer conflicts over food when the atmosphere has been that of a social occasion. Happy meal tables have been those where conversation was encouraged, along with eating, where children were allowed to express preferences over food and there was not the insistence that they finish every last morsel.

Alternatively, I have sat, with increasing shock, at meal tables where from practically the first mouthful there was a barrage from workers of 'Well, I hope you're going to eat up properly today!', 'Come on, hurry up!' and 'Eat up that cabbage or no pudding for you!' Insensitive and impatient adults were not putting themselves in the children's shoes for one moment. Such continual nagging would lead the most patient adult to say 'You can keep your dinner!'

Unfair judgements on children

Toilet training

There is no point in getting angry with children who are toilet-trained but still have accidents from time to time. If the accidents are happening because of anxiety or absorption in play, then adult anger is only likely to make the situation worse. It is reasonable for you to communicate to a child that you would rather they made it to the toilet in time, but this has to be in the context that you want to help this to happen.

When children have accidents it can be a positive move to involve them in finding clean clothes and fetching a mop (if needed) but this action is in the spirit of saying they are old enough to help you; it is not a punishment. Shouting at children or humiliating them for such accidents is cruel and does not help the problem. Children do not usually wet or soil themselves out of defiance and the few who do use this action to punish adults are more likely to be pleased than daunted by adult anger.

Some children who become absorbed in their play ignore, until it is too late, the physical feelings that signal they need to go to the toilet. It can help to remind children discreetly or take them to the bathroom at regular intervals. Be encouraging when children monitor their own needs and calm when they do not.

Learning confusions
Children are learning a stunning array of new ideas and it would be most surprising if there were not some confusions sometimes (see page 74, for example). When children are having troubles learning there is no point in adults' becoming irritated and no justification to decide that a child is being deliberately awkward. Such adult unreasonableness will only make children more anxious, likely to cover up their lack of understanding and to withdraw from a learning activity. The most likely explanation for blank looks or odd answers is that children do not understand, or possibly that they have not learned to attend well (see page 67). Both possible explanations imply some change in adult's behaviour.

CHILDREN IN DISTRESS

Children who withdraw
Some children are a concern because they are too quiet. They may spend a lot of time rocking alone or thumb-sucking. Or they may be children who wander aimlessly around a nursery class or playgroup, perhaps staring or just following other children or adults.

There are undoubtedly children who enjoy playing alone for some of their time and many children go through temporary unhappy times. However, if you observe children, you will soon distinguish the self-sufficient child or the one who is temporarily out of sorts from the child who is frequently withdrawn and isolated (see page 52 for observation techniques). It is important to keep an eye on the overly quiet child and not to miss a child who needs help because you are thinking of a very quiet child as a 'good' or well-behaved member of the group. A very quiet child may also be dismissed by inexperienced or insensitive workers as a dull child who shows no interest.

- Very quiet children may be experiencing a number of different emotions. They may be unhappy or depressed and the main cause may be within or outside the setting.
- Other children may be very shy and ill-at-ease in a group. Some children can be disconcerted by the numbers of other children and adults in a large nursery or playgroup
- Disorientated and withdrawn children sometimes do not know how to play. Perhaps they have had little contact with other children or are concerned about not behav-

ing wrongly in the group. Perhaps this child has little previous experience of play or of this array of play materials.

When a child in your care seems very quiet, you should seek a conversation with the parents – not necessarily assuming that something is wrong – but in order to gain some perspective on whether what you are observing is usual for this child. Clearly a great deal depends on the individual child. Some children, for instance, faced with a novel range of play materials, go a little wild and rush around from one activity to another. They may also need help to settle.

Bringing out the quiet child
Your approach to a very quiet child will have to be gradual. You have to be patient and willing to give a lot of time to a child before a response may follow. If the child's main difficulty stems from lack of play experience, then regular periods of time spent with her will help her to settle. Perhaps you will show her how to use one kind of activity or equipment each day and ease her entry into groups of other children.

A child whose extreme quietness is a response to neglect or a continuing unhappy home life may be very unresponsive to your friendly overtures. You may begin to feel inadequate since an encouraging approach that has worked with other children seems to be getting you nowhere. Sometimes, you have to be pleased with very small steps of progress, for instance that a child has become comfortable with your playing alongside but she is not yet ready to respond to any of your comments. Your continued friendly presence, a shared interesting activity and no pressure may gradually build up a sense of trust.

A very quiet child may not know how to approach adults or may be very wary of any adult because of her previous experiences. Expressions of friendliness and affection will help to establish a good relationship so long as you are patient in expecting a response. Physical affection and cuddling may win a child's confidence but should not ever be imposed. Be guided by individual children; some appreciate a friendly touch or cuddle more than others.

When you are working to bring a very quiet child out of her shell, you have to accept that a likely consequence is that the child will become most attached to one adult, at least in the short term. Part of that adult's task will be later to help the child to approach other adults and mix with children. However, the process is likely to take some time until the child gains the confidence to leave the protection of the single trusted adult.

Child abuse and child protection

Children who have been on the receiving end of physical, sexual or emotional abuse will be distressed and the experience will emerge in some way through their behaviour. Some of the behaviour described within this chapter might be shown by children who have been abused by parents, other relatives or persons known to the family. But not all children who show distress, or whose behaviour worries you, will have been abused.

Every early years setting should have a policy understood by all workers on what steps are to be taken if child abuse is suspected. You need to discuss any such concerns about a child with the manager of your setting and should neither question children nor undertake any investigation on your own.

You need to be observant and realise that child abuse does occur across the social and ethnic spectrum, but you should never come to the swift conclusion that child abuse has occurred.

- You are looking far more for patterns of behaviour rather than single incidents. There is no neat list of children's actions that indicate abuse, although some behaviour, for example sexually explicit physical contact or language from a young child, should trigger serious concern.
- You should always allow parents to give an explanation for odd marks or bruises. You would be angry if parents' immediate reaction to accidents in your setting were to report you for abuse.
- If children tell you something that implies that they have been abused, then you should take them seriously. But you still cannot assume, without further discussion and observation, that what they are telling you is the full picture.

This section gives only a brief coverage of an important topic. You will find useful references in the 'Suggested Reading' section on page 164.

Helping children in distress

When to worry about a child
Children who are temporarily upset may retreat into themselves and most children have some way of comforting themselves in times of trouble: thumb or finger-sucking, a favourite teddy or a piece of blanket. This kind of behaviour should not concern adults. You can offer comfort and attention, as well as be pleased that children also have their own means of comfort.

You should be concerned for children who withdraw into self-absorbed and repetitive behaviour that isolates them in their own personal world for much of the time. Children should concern you who:

- Rock and hold themselves close for long periods of time and are reluctant to accept comfort and be drawn out.
- Pick at their skin so as to create sore spots, pull their hair out or any kind of behaviour that results in deliberate self-injury.
- Bang their heads against anything, even if it is another person and not a hard surface.

- Play with their genitals a great deal or for long periods of time. Children sometimes slip a hand into their pants as a temporary form of comfort. You would discourage them from doing this in public, since it is not acceptable social behaviour for older children, but would not worry if all else was well.
- Say anything to you that suggests they have very low self-esteem, especially repeated remarks that 'I'm no good' or 'Nobody likes me'. Never ignore any comments such as 'I wish I was dead' – children do not make this kind of remark as part of a phase.

Talking with parents
If you are concerned about a child who behaves in any of the above ways, you will be taking a positive approach to her within your setting (some practical suggestions follow) but you should also talk with her parent(s). You need time for a proper conversation and in private, not snatched moments within hearing of other parents and children. Family crisis may be affecting the parents as well as the child and your support may be welcome, even when you can do nothing about the causes of the crisis. Your important role can also be, with sensitivity, to report to absorbed adults that their child is reacting badly to events. Parents under stress are not necessarily abusing their child (see also the preceding section) but they may have lost sight of her emotional needs. Any approach you take to support a child away from compulsive or self-harming behaviour will be that much more effective if you and the parent(s) are working together.

Acting to help a child
Simply telling children to stop rocking or playing with themselves is unlikely to achieve much because you are asking them to give up the one action that is currently enabling them to cope. It will be more effective to help the child express their feelings and to offer alternative forms of comfort – from an adult, the company of other children and play which is not so withdrawn and compulsive.

Make time to be close to the child, so far as she will tolerate. Talk quietly with her and offer activities in which you are also involved. She may not want physical contact, such as sitting very close or holding your hand but be close enough so that you can gently stop the rocking or scratching. If you continue to spend regular periods of time with a child, or you and a colleague share this effort, you will gradually interest the child in yourself, what you are saying, or maybe in singing to her and then some peaceful play activities. Perhaps the child will be happy to look at a picture book with you, maybe cuddling a toy or blanket for comfort, or she may wish to become involved with your own routine activities and just be with you.

This process is likely to take time because children do not just snap out of sad and depressed states. Children need your time, patience and caring attention. They certainly do not need criticism or harsh words, which will only drive them further into themselves.

Children who are physically harming themselves through head-banging or fierce hair-pulling need to be stopped but you will need to do more than say 'Don't do that'. The feelings underlying head-banging can be anger, frustration or despair. Some children with severe learning disabilities seem to head-bang as the means of creating strong sensations. Even limited head-banging is best discouraged because children can hurt themselves. Serious head-bangers can badly harm themselves.

It is often possible to place a hand between the child's head and the surface against which he is banging. You can both protect the child's head and gently lift him back upright. A firm 'No', as you place your hand, can get the child's attention. Reassure or comfort the child as appropriate, perhaps talk with him and ideally involve him in some activity with you. A firm 'No'; and a hand clap may get the child's attention from across the room and give you time to get across to him. If you persevere there is a good chance that the child will begin to stop herself, often with the same word or phrase that you have used. In a similar way, you can discourage a child from pulling out her own hair or picking at her skin by gently moving her hand away. Depending on the child, you might encourage her to express her feelings through words, drawing or make-believe play.

If you are unable to discourage any self-harming habit in a relatively short time (or at least see a noticeable reduction) then do suggest to the parents that they should consult a Child Psychologist.

Wanting to act like a younger child

Children sometimes regress in their behaviour and for a short or longer period of time they behave as they did when they were younger.

Children who are adjusting to the arrival of a new baby sometimes insist on returning to their previous baby ways, perhaps wanting a bottle when they have managed well with a cup for some time. This change in behaviour is not surprising since the older child sees the baby receiving attention for being little and helpless. The older one may feel for a while that the compensations of being older and more able than the baby do not make up for having to share a parent's attention. Sensitive help from parents and other carers can help older children to enjoy what they can do, including help with the baby as far as they want. If the temporary regression to baby ways is tolerated without criticism and children's more mature accomplishments are encouraged, then they will begin to act their age.

Regressions can happen in toilet-training, eating or any other area in which children are learning to cope on their own. It is neither helpful nor fair to children to label their actions as 'naughty'; competent children will have reasons for acting immaturely. Perhaps they are checking that they can be babied if they wish or adults may have, perhaps unintentionally, put too much pressure on a child to act as the 'big girl' now.

Sometimes, illness leads children to want the kind of reassurance and comforting that was usual when they were younger.

Remember that, for all their leaps in development, five and six-year-olds are still young in many ways. There will be times when they could manage something on their own, but at this moment they want an adult to help them or do it for them. As long as this is not becoming a helpless outlook, then it is fine to indulge children sometimes. After all, most adults are capable of making themselves a cup of coffee or a snack but it is very pleasant to have someone do this for you as an occasional treat.

Fears and worries

Most children are frightened by some event at some time: a character or scene in a video (even those made for young children), a loud barking dog or a squeaky door. You should take children's concerns seriously but without agreeing necessarily that this is dangerous or frightening and certainly without feeding the fear. For instance, some children see worrying patterns in their curtains or wallpaper, especially in the half-light. You should not dismiss the fear as 'silly'. Accept what the child says she sees but explain about how things can look funny in the dark and try to find some happy or good images in the wallpaper. If children are frightened of worms or caterpillars, you can reassure them that these creatures do not hurt and perhaps help the children to learn more about how worms help in the garden.

Give children a chance to talk about what makes them uneasy and then you may be able to reassure them. Perhaps it will help to know that worms are not the same as snakes or that caterpillars will not be able to climb into the bedroom window. If the children want to overcome their uneasiness then you can help but there is nothing to be gained by thrusting worms at them on the grounds that 'they ought to get over it!'. After all, many adults are frightened of small creatures such as spiders or mice. If a child is frightened of dogs you may help her deal with the general fear by your reassuring presence whilst leaving her with a healthy respect for unknown dogs.

Many children are wary of the dark and it can be at bedtime that fears become real that remain at bay during the daylight hours. My own daughter, when young, loved watching an animated version of 'The Wind in the Willows' but was very uneasy about the weasels and sure they would appear in her bedroom. In a family home, or a residential home, there is no justification for insisting that children sleep in the complete dark. Children's bedrooms should feel safe and welcoming to them and a night light or low-wattage bulb in an ordinary light can make all the difference to an uneasy child. Children may also need reassurance about vague fears of monsters or burglars under the bed. You can reassure a child that this is not the case but respect their feelings by checking the bed or cupboard.

When fears take over

For some children their fears become a major influence in their lives and can turn into phobias. The difference is that fears are experienced about something that a child is feeling or seeing at the time. If the feelings become worse then the fear may be provoked by the possibility of encountering what frightens them or entire days are overcast by the prospect of going to bed and the monsters. A child who hesitates by a gate where a dog has previously leapt out is reacting to a concrete fear. However, if she starts to resist leaving home because the dogs are lying in wait for her, then the fear may be dominating her life. Complex rituals to avoid a fear are also a warning sign that the fear, or the way of coping, is getting out of hand. If the child's life, and that of her family, is being very disrupted by the fear then it may be time to seek outside advice, for example that of a Child Psychologist.

A life full of real danger

Some children have lives that are genuinely full of frightening events and threatening people. A family may have very aggressive neighbours, the estate may be genuinely dangerous or the family may be on the receiving end of racist abuse. Children who live in fear react differently. Some retreat in on themselves but some deal with the pressure by being indiscriminately aggressive to other children. If children have learned to behave in this way, you have to be very patient in building trust and creating a secure atmosphere for them. You need to discourage the aggression but knowledge of the child's life can help you to see that the attacks are not really personal.

ADULTS' AND CHILDREN'S BEHAVIOUR

A positive approach to children and what they do has to include consideration of the adults involved. Nobody is usually helped by attempts to assign blame as such, but adult behaviour is definitely an ingredient in the situation and cannot be ignored, as if every difficulty arises only from the children. No adult, however experienced, will get it right all the time and with every child. Part of a positive approach to children has to be an adult willingness to stand back, think over possibilities and admit in a constructive way that the current approach is not really helping. Recognition of the fact that you could adjust will not only help children but will leave you in a position to continue to learn.

SUGGESTED FURTHER READING

Bee, Helen (1997) *The Developing Child*. Longman.

Dreikurs, Rudolf (1981) *Happy Children: A Challenge to Parents*. Fontana.

Hartley-Brewer, Elizabeth (1994) *Positive Parenting: Raising Children with Self-Esteem*. Cedar.

Leach, Penelope (1992) *Young Children under Stress*. National Early Years Network – Starting Points No. 13.

Miedzian, Myriam (1992) *Boys Will be Boys: Breaking the Link Between Masculinity and Violence*. Virago.

Pearce, John (1989) *Worries and Fears*. Thorsons. There are several other titles in this practical series.

Rogers, Bill (1993) *You Know the Fair Rule: Strategies for Making the Hard Job of Discipline in School Easier*. Longman.

Schaffer, H. Rudolph (1990) *Making Decisions about Children: Psychological Questions and Answers*. Basil Blackwell.

Slaby, Ronald G. and others (1995) *Early Violence Prevention: Tools for Teachers of Young Children*. National Association for the Education of Young Children. (Available from the National Early Years Network.)

Wilson, Avril and Joseph, Yvonne (1996) *Recognising Child Abuse: A Guide for Early Years Workers*. National Early Years Network – Starting Points No. 6.

The following organisation is an excellent resource for books and leaflets on using encouragement and consequences: Adlerian Workshops and Publications, 216 Tring Road, Aylesbury, Bucks. HP20 1JS, Tel: 01296 82148

PART 4

PARTNERSHIP
WITH PARENTS

10

PARTNERSHIP WITHIN EARLY YEARS WORK

Adult involvement in children's lives

Young children usually have several key adults in their lives. Some of these adults are relatives and some will be family friends. In different ways, the adults whose lives touch those of children are faced with the business of working well together within a family or friendship network. They are also faced with the consequences for themselves and the children of not working together.

As parents stop taking sole responsibility for their children, then other adults – nursery and playgroup workers, childminders, nannies – become involved in the children's lives. They all share an adult status but their roles are different. They have come together over the heads of the children and the adults have to sort out their respective roles for the well-being of the children.

A HISTORICAL PERSPECTIVE

Partnership with parents is regarded as an integral part of good practice in early years services and education, and to a greater or lesser extent in other services for families. Partnership is such a common part of policy statements or the written material given to parents by early years settings that it is easy to forget that an active attempt to work with parents was not always part of the professional approach. The development of partnership – and it works in very different ways in different settings – was influenced by several broad social changes and shifts in professional thinking.

Involving parents to help with children's difficulties

The early years intervention programmes of the 1960s were based in the perspective that children's potential was strongly influenced by their environment and that there was a social responsibility to help them to achieve that potential. A number of the projects for disadvantaged children, in America and Britain, indicated that the impact of any work lasted longer if parents were closely involved in the project.

Over a similar period of time, there was a growing emphasis in social work and social psychiatry that difficulties experienced by children could not sensibly be seen in isolation from their family. This approach led to attempts to work with parents as well as children and to draw parents into settings such as family centres. Both this approach and the conclusions drawn from intervention projects were an encouragement to involving parents because they were seen as essential to improve the prospects of their children. In some cases, parents were seen as part of the problem.

Sharing skills with parents to help children

Through the 1970s there was a growing realism among some professionals that they were unlikely to progress much with children on the basis of infrequent specialist sessions. Far more progress was likely if parents could understand the process and continue any special work with children at home. A number of specialist units with children, for instance the Hester Adrian Centre in Manchester and the Wolfson Clinic in London, built into any programme a positive contact with parents who were given specific practical suggestions to undertake between sessions. Home visiting schemes, such as the Portage programme for children with learning or physical disabilities, took this approach one step further by shifting the specialist input to visits in the family home. The assumption underlying any work of this kind was that many parents would be motivated and able to become involved in a process that was helping their child.

Involvement of parents in programmes for their children is so usual now that it is all too easy to forget that many professionals resisted any level of involvement from the conviction that parents had no skills and would inevitably interfere and block the professional input. A different example within the same theme is the change in approach over children bringing reading books home from school. It is now very common to see nursery, reception and primary school age children with their reading folders. But the first experiments in this particular home-school link, in the 1970s, were faced with strong resistance from teachers, convinced that parents would approach reading in all the wrong ways and disturb the process as taught within school.

Parents as people with rights and responsibilities

The development of partnership was sometimes led more by concern about problems for children and in families than from any strong sense that a good relationship with parents should be part of the work of any professional involved with children.

An alternative perspective emerged from growing pressure that parents had a right to be involved and consulted since they were users of a public service – day care or education. Organisations such as the Advisory Centre for Education were influential in establishing a view that parents had every right to information about their children's schooling because they were responsible for their children. This theme of consumer, or service-user, rights has continued against a social background of greater awareness of the responsibilities and accountability of anyone who runs a service.

The series of Parents' Charters during the 1990s established the framework that all parents had the right to certain expectations for their children's education, clear information and the means to challenge decisions. The Children Act of 1989 also confirmed a framework in which professionals involved with families were expected to work in partnership with parents, or other relatives taking parental responsibility.

Parents with skills and experience to offer

The move by groups of professionals to share skills with parents was based in a belief that parents were able and keen to help their children. Active parents' groups also worked to challenge the restrictive view that professionals in early years – or any other children's services – were the people with expertise and that parents had nothing special to offer; they were 'just parents'.

The playgroup movement from the 1960s took what was then a radical approach in involving parents, mainly mothers, in the daily running and sometimes the management of the playgroups. Other early years settings have followed with different kinds of involvement, many of which assume that parents have skills and expertise. A strong theme in the practical application of equal opportunities on ethnic group, culture and religion has been to tap the resources of parents' own experience.

BREADTH IN PARTNERSHIP

Early years settings vary considerably in their organisation, the focus of their work and the families who attend. So, it is not surprising that partnership in action can, and probably should, look very different in the varied settings. Parents are offered a role or encouraged to become involved in early years settings in all of the following ways. Practice is not the same in every setting and from page 172 you will find a discussion of how genuine partnership with parents may work in action.

First contacts

Many early years settings have a pattern for contact between parents and staff before a child's first official day. This can include any of the following:

- An invitation for parents, probably with their children, to visit before taking up the offer of a place.
- Written material in the form of a leaflet for parents about the setting and expectations.
- A meeting to clarify the conditions under which a child, and perhaps the parents too in a family centre, will attend. A written agreement or contract may then be signed by parents and the head of centre.
- A visit by staff to the family home. This may be usual procedure for some children's centres and family centres.

Continuing communication between parents and workers

Partnership has in many early years settings come to be seen as part of a continuing, friendly relationship between the centre and parents. Communication may be achieved through any of the following:

- Daily, face-to-face contact as parents bring and pick up children.
- Informally arranged conversations about children along the lines of 'Can I have a word about . . .', asked by staff or parents.
- Regular meetings with parents to discuss children's progress, and not just to be called when there are problems.
- A clear procedure to enable parents to look at their own child's files.
- Invitations to parents to attend medicals, reviews and any other meeting or special help for their child.
- Open days or evenings for parents to see their own child's work and the general approach of the setting to children's learning.
- A notice board, newsletter or other general means of communication with parents.

Support for activities within the setting

Partnership may also be put into practice by inviting, or expecting, parents to become involved in a range of activities or events.

- As organisers or supporters of fund-raising events.
- Sharing responsibility for a continuing activity such as running the toy library.
- Collecting materials for use by children in their play. For instance, materials for junk modelling.

Parents present within the day or session

A positive approach to parents as useful and not interfering individuals led to considerably more presence of parents within the normal running of nurseries and other centres. The playgroup movement pioneered this type of involvement but other settings followed suit. The variety includes:

- Staying to settle a child into the early years centre. Again, this approach is so much part of normal practice now that it is easy to forget that up to the late 1970s, at least, it was far more usual that children started on a given day, parents waved goodbye and that was that.
- Parents welcome to stay with their (now settled) child, to join children for tea or other social events.
- Parents as helpers within the daily activities of the group or helping out on special occasions like trips.

A welcoming centre may have many parents who are pleased to spend time with you.

Parents as part of their children's learning

Partnership with parents also extends in some settings to working with them to support children's learning – either within the usual curriculum or on special programmes for individual children.

- Continuing programmes of work or projects at home, including home and school reading links.
- Parents may be present with their child in the setting and part of the play activities. This pattern is more likely to be set up when staff are concerned to help a parent to learn how to play with or relate positively to their child.

Social activities for parents as adults

Some settings have developed partnership through social events arranged for parents, primarily in their role as adults, who might welcome company:

- Hospitality for parents to stay in the setting and have informal social contact with other parents or workers, or arranged events, such as coffee mornings.
- An on-going parents' group, club or room for the exclusive use of parents and other carers.
- Social events that may also be fund-raisers such as barbecues or dances.
- Access to sessions that interest parents, such as craft groups, learning second and third languages or outside speakers on topics that interest parents, not necessarily about children.

Help for parents as adults

Some early years settings offer specific help to parents:

- Advice and support in parenting and child care – either through informal individual contact or a parents' group.
- Resources of information and general advice, staff willing to act as an advocate for parents in contacting and dealing with official bodies.
- Help with problems, not necessarily on parenting, that may move towards offering a counselling relationship in the setting.

A role in policy and decision-making

There are two aspects of this side of partnership:

- Parents having an active role and the necessary information to participate in decisions about their own child.
- Parent involvement in the broader running of a setting – for example parent representatives on management committees or parent governors in schools.

A FRAMEWORK FOR PARTNERSHIP

There are certain qualities essential to a real partnership with parents and these are well described by the following quotation. Partnership is:

> **A working relationship that is characterised by a shared sense of purpose, mutual respect and the willingness to negotiate. This implies a sharing of information, responsibility, skills, decision making and accountability.**

> *From Gillian Pugh and Erica De'Ath, Working Towards Partnership in the Early Years (1989)*

A continuing process

None of the examples above are necessarily better illustrations of partnership than any other. The essence of good practice in this area is not so much the particular approach to partnership but how a staff team reached the decision about what partnership would mean in this setting and exactly how they behave towards parents through their chosen approach.

What could be a very positive choice in one setting might be irresponsible in another setting with different resources, staff skills and body of parents. For example, a programme that required working parents to take time off work to attend many events during the day has not been developed in the spirit of partnership. Two similar settings might carry out plans that look the same on paper but the two staff groups behave so differently towards parents that a lack of respect in one setting creates a programme that has none of the features of partnership experienced in the second.

Partnership in its different forms is not an optional extra in early years services – tacked on to existing patterns. A genuine partnership between workers and parents requires some hard thinking by workers and often a reappraisal of their role. The thinking, talking and consulting with parents will continue, since partnership is not something you fix and then leave, like a leaking roof.

The nature of partnership

Some of the variety between settings develops from the different adults involved – parents and staff – and the setting's resources. But some differences undoubtedly develop because of how the adults involved are viewing the possibilities of partnership. When thinking over partnership within early years settings there are two perspectives which are especially relevant: the balance of power and the nature of exchanges between staff and parents. Beliefs about these two broad issues influence judgements made by both staff and parents about how relationships ought to develop, what is appropriate and what is not ever considered as a possibility.

Power and balance of power
The essence of a partnership is that there is some equality of power between the parties. The pattern of rights, responsibilities and expertise that makes up power are not likely to be the same between parents and workers; they are in different positions and roles.

A series of questions follows which can help you to think about the balance of power in your own early years setting:

- Whose views count most in discussions of the curriculum and methods of helping children to learn? What happens if parents express doubts or openly disagree with centre methods? Partnership might be said to be working when parents feel able to ask awkward questions.
- How are decisions made in this setting and what is the level of parent representation on decision-making bodies?
- Who determines what range of activities is offered in the spirit of partnership (see

page 169 for a wide range) and whose judgement counts in assessing to what extent these are successful?

- How is the role determined of parents who are present during the day, for instance as a parent-helper?
- Who decides how parents are given access to their children's files? (An obstructive system of delays can communicate very clearly that power over information rests with the staff.)

There may always be some imbalance between staff and parents. One issue is that all the staff are responsible for following the policies that underpin practice in the setting. They cannot flex on key principles, however strongly a parent might feel to the contrary. So one could say that the balance of power in this aspect to practice is weighted towards the staff. Yet, partnership can be maintained through clear and honest information with explanation.

A second issue is that, realistically, parents may be loath to vote with their feet if they are dissatisfied with some aspect of the setting. There may not be any viable alternative nursery, playgroup or school to which the child can be transferred. Again partnership can be developed by staff who do not exploit the lack of alternatives for parents through a 'take it or leave it' attitude, and who certainly do not load their disagreements with a parent onto the child .

One- or two-way exchange between parents and staff
A second important dimension to a real partnership is the extent to which communication and sharing between staff and parents is largely one-way (from staff to parents) or a more balanced and reciprocal, two-way exchange. The questions for you to consider here are given in pairs. Use them to think seriously about your own outlook on partnership as well as the broader pattern in your setting.

- What do you believe parents could learn from the workers in your staff team?
- What do you believe staff could learn from parents?

- What information would you like from parents that they are not sharing at the moment?
- Ask parents what information they would like from you that is not being shared, or not easily, at present.

- What do you think that parents really need to understand to be in tune with the aims and practice of your setting?
- What do staff really need to grasp about the family life and pressures of individual parents?

- As a worker, what would you like parents to respect about your professional expertise?

- What would parents like staff to respect about their abilities and expertise?

- From the staff perspective, how could parents make life easier for you? What would you like them to start doing or stop doing?
- In what ways could staff make life easier for parents? What would parents most like you to start or stop doing?

You will be able to explore some of these paired questions within your staff group but some will require you to talk with parents in an open way and look through their eyes.

PLANNING TO DEVELOP PARTNERSHIP

An essential part of partnership is consultation with parents, but this communication may become muddled while a staff group is confused or in disagreement amongst themselves over the meaning of partnership in their setting. It is certainly unwise to approach the development of partnership with the stance of 'What shall we do and how fast can we get started?'

Your aims for partnership

You need to be clear as an individual worker about your general aims but the staff team of which you are a member also needs to have a shared view of aims, which may of course develop and change over time. The aims of different early years settings can vary and could include any of the following general aims:

- We want parents to understand better what we do with the children during a session.
- We want parents to have a better relationship with their own children.
- We want to support parents in specialised work with their children.
- We would like to benefit from parents' knowledge and experience.
- We want parents to share the responsibility for decisions within the centre.
- We would like to offer help to parents for their problems.
- We want parents to recognise the pressures we are under and not make things worse for us.

Any aims should be discussed thoroughly within your own team so that you consider your statements from alternative perspectives. For instance, a useful discussion might follow the two sets of questions about balance of power and a two-way exchange. The aims given above appear to take different stances on those issues. Another way to gain perspective on what may be only the staff view is to imagine your aims written up on a large poster in a public area of your setting. Aims such as 'helping parents to improve their relationship with their children' can sound feasible in staff meetings but would look decidedly arrogant on public display.

Planning, discussion and consultation in partnership

Staff planning and discussion   *Consultation with parents*

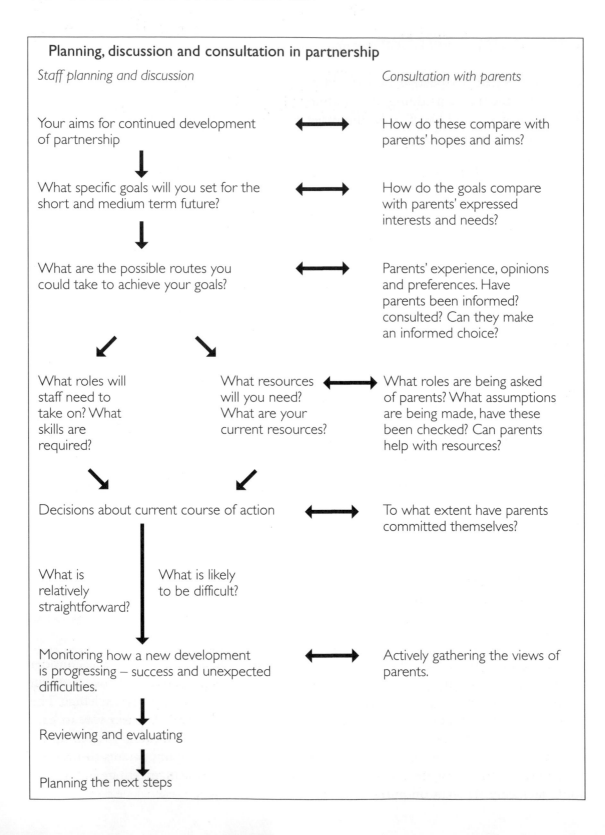

Your aims for continued development of partnership ⟷ How do these compare with parents' hopes and aims?

What specific goals will you set for the short and medium term future? ⟷ How do the goals compare with parents' expressed interests and needs?

What are the possible routes you could take to achieve your goals? ⟷ Parents' experience, opinions and preferences. Have parents been informed? consulted? Can they make an informed choice?

What roles will staff need to take on? What skills are required?

What resources will you need? What are your current resources? ⟶ What roles are being asked of parents? What assumptions are being made, have these been checked? Can parents help with resources?

Decisions about current course of action ⟷ To what extent have parents committed themselves?

What is relatively straightforward?

What is likely to be difficult?

Monitoring how a new development is progressing – success and unexpected difficulties. ⟷ Actively gathering the views of parents.

Reviewing and evaluating

Planning the next steps

Useful goals

Aims can be vague and general descriptions or aspirations; goals are set to bring a definite framework for practice. A staff team needs to look in detail at the setting's aims and ask 'How will we judge we are achieving this aim when we see it?' This discussion about 'what will be happening?' and 'how will the setting change?' will take you towards a discussion of goals.

Goals define a particular point or state you want to reach and not how you reach it. So a goal is not 'We'll have an open evening and tell parents why we don't teach children to read in the nursery'. The goal hidden in this definite action plan is the wish to have parents understand your methods, perhaps so they stop complaining 'Why don't you teach them to read and write?' An open evening may not be the best way to deal with the different perspectives of parents and staff and that particular plan includes the unspoken assumption that the parents do not have a valid point.

To be of any real help to you, goals in any plan need to have the following qualities.

Specific
Goals need to be worded in such a way that you can tell whether or not they have been achieved. Aims may be more vague, while goals have to be definite.

Observable
You have to be able to observe the progress you have made in a goal, to measure (not in a complex way) how far you have moved, what has happened and what has not. Goals are not helpful if they include phrases like 'as far as possible' or 'we'll try to . . .' because these cautionary clauses undermine any definite intent.

Realistic
For everyone's sake goals must be within the bounds of possibility; it must be likely that they could be achieved within the short or medium-term future. A goal that is unlikely to be reached relatively soon or that requires many other changes is far better redrafted as a number of goals that recognise the steps along the way.

Time-bound
Part of practical goals in your setting will be a commitment to 'by when?' Discussion about a time limit for likely achievement of a goal or of reviewing progress can focus attention on whether the goal is realistic. A built-in time limit will also prevent loss of energy and interest as a goal about partnership (or anything else) rolls on into the future.

Involvement
Individuals who are responsible for goals need to feel personally involved and committed. This is equally true for parents as for staff. Anyone is far more likely to become

involved if they are part of the discussion that sets these goals and have therefore been properly consulted.

Any of these qualities of a useful goals are equally applicable to goals in your work with children, see page 8.

Example: Rhiannon Nursery School

The nursery school team are in the process of working towards more partnership with parents. Their overall aim was to be able to write honestly on the nursery brochure that 'We run Rhiannon Nursery School in partnership with parents'. In a series of staff meetings they have repeatedly addressed the question of 'How will we recognise partnership as it develops?' and 'What do we think partnership really is in our setting?' They reached a set of draft goals that there would be a developing partnership when:

1 There is a change in how we run the nursery that comes from an idea contributed by a parent.
2 We try to have at least one parent in the building all day long each day.
3 Staff ask parents for their views and really listen.
4 An event in the nursery is planned and run completely by parents.
5 Parents understand what we are trying to do and we understand what they are trying to do.

In fact the five items are not yet workable goals but further discussion in the team about each item highlights further understanding of the process of partnership. For instance, items 1 and 4 lead to discussion about 'what kind of change or event?' and the recognition that however strongly parents might feel they could not be permitted to bring about a change that went contrary to nursery policy and principles such as equal opportunities. Items 3 and 5 lead to discussion about what gets in the way of listening to each other or understanding an alternative perspective. Item 2 raises the issue that 'trying' is not the point; if the goal is worthwhile then staff want to achieve it, not just try.

Possible routes to achieve a goal

Once a staff team, or a collaborative group such as a management committee, has practical goals to which they can work then it is feasible to look at possible routes to achieve those goals. It is best to consider possibilities in an open-ended way and not to assume that another setting's methods will necessarily suit your own setting. The next boxed example takes on the illustration from the Rhiannon Nursery School.

> **Example: Consultation with parents on changes**
>
> After discussion the team at Rhiannon Nursery School have developed their first draft goal into 'We will consult parents on their views for any major changes in the nursery'. The possibilities for the spare room are the first focus for consultation with parents. The team are clear that they wish to hear parents' views but are aware that there are several ways in which they could encourage consultation. They discuss the pros and cons of the following methods:
>
> * They could ask every parent individually.
> * There is a parents' notice board in the hallway and a notice could be pinned up, asking for suggestions.
> * A meeting could be held on the topic of the spare room.
> * The possibility of some kind of regular consultation is raised again – whether the nursery should have a parent-staff forum or something similar.

Assessment of resources

For any goal, in partnership or other developments in your setting, there will be more than one possible route. You need to consider each possibility and weigh up the question of:

* What resources do we need for this particular development? What do we have?

The resources of any setting will provide positives and negatives. It is important not to highlight the perceived negatives ('We haven't got a spare room to make into a parents' room') and overlook the positives ('At least six different ethnic groups are represented in the parents. They have specialist knowledge to complement staff skills and a quarter of the parents are bilingual').

Any setting will have different kinds of resources, some of which may be overlooked or under-used:

* The building(s) and the spaces available, including different use of available space.
* The people: staff and parents (skills, talent, time and energy) and the broader network that can be reached through them.
* Finance: available funds and the options for raising more money through grants or fund-raising events.
* Access to additional facilities, equipment, transport and the like.

Sometimes there will be a gap between your current resources and what is realistically needed for your preferred plan of action. If the gap is wide and not easy to close in the near future, then a different plan will be advisable for now, with efforts to find more resources for the longer-term.

Different courses of action will also require consideration of:

- What role does this require of staff and how different is the role from what happens at the moment? What skills are required and to what extent can we meet this currently?
- Development of a partnership approach requires a very different outlook from a stance that views early years professionals as the ones with the expertise. New developments may require staff to become comfortable in the role of partner, whilst remaining clear about their professional obligations and the setting's policies.

Generally, you need to discuss and assess:

- Overall what will help us to work towards and achieve this goal?
- What may hinder us and how can we overcome any problems?

Example: Boundaries Playgroup

Boundaries was originally set up in the expectation that all parents would take a turn on the rota. This compulsory system was dropped when it became clear that parents with jobs could not easily meet the requirement and that unwilling parents were not useful helpers. Some years have passed and Marion, the playgroup leader, has been looking at re-introducing parent-helpers on a voluntary basis. The idea arose in staff discussion of the goal of offering help to parents who seemed uncertain how to play with their children. Some parents have also started to stay for sessions informally.

The playgroup team are aware that they need to be clear about what they are offering to parents before they move from the informal conversations so far held with parents towards proper consultation. Marion also wishes to be clear about the playgroup's plans so that she can present them at the next management committee meeting.

So far the playgroup team have generated a 'think about' list that includes:

- Check on our resources: how many adults can we comfortably (and safely) have in the playgroup at any one time? Do we need to know who is coming to which session? How will the children react if there is uncertainty?
- Can we offer proper hospitality to parent-helpers – enough coffee cups? Our toilets are unisex, is this going to bother anyone? How can we put parent-helpers at ease – our social skills?
- Practical issues such as insurance – check on the details. What if a parent is injured in the playgroup or a child in the responsibility of a parent-helper? Are there responsibilities that must not be given to parent-helpers?

- How may we need to adjust our role: to guide parent-helpers so they act within our policies and methods with the children? To support parents who want to learn how to play with children or to manage their own child more positively?
- Are we clear about our reasons for inviting parents in as helpers? Do parents understand our approach and do we understand their motivation for wanting to help? Different parents may have different reasons for joining us and we do not share a language with all the parents.
- We need to be aware of how we feel about having parents more present in the playgroup and have the opportunity to talk about our (dis)comfort with each other.

Questions:
You might like to try a similar list of practical questions for a different development in partnership, perhaps home visits to families or running a group for parents within your setting.

Continuing development in partnership

If you have set yourself practical and specific goals then it will be clear as you make progress towards those goals. The process continues since partnership, like the application of equal opportunities in early years work, is not something you achieve and then nothing else changes. Both these important principles are part of a continuing process.

Specific goals can be very positive since they support staff in finding satisfaction in their work; there is a sense of achievement and progress. Sometimes goals will not be achieved, perhaps because of unexpected difficulties or issues that could not realistically have been predicted. Teams can learn from frustrations and the need to re-draft goals or a plan of action. Perhaps enthusiasm to get going and being seen to be doing something led a team to rush through without proper consultation with parents or with limited resources. Team leaders and centre managers can be crucial in offering support to frustrated or disheartened staff and in ensuring that lessons are learned.

It is worth keeping records of different developments in partnership with parents. Some forms of involvement for parents may be heavily used by only a few but this may be judged to be appropriate. On the other hand, meetings that bring only a handful of parents may be under-used because the topic or approach is of no interest or practical issues have been overlooked – for instance that short notice made it impossible for parents to get sitters to emerge for an evening. Certainly it would be unjustified to assume that parents are 'not interested' because they have chosen not to follow a particular route towards partnership that was determined, without consultation, by the staff.

THE PERSPECTIVE OF PARENTS

It is inevitable that staff approach partnership from a different perspective to parents, even when those staff have children of their own and are therefore parents in another part of their life. Different perspectives are not necessarily a problem so long as staff and parents both talk and listen to each other. The diagram on page 176 shows how consultation with parents is crucial at every point in any plans for developing or expanding partnership. Staff need to ask themselves questions about 'What do parents prefer?', 'What do they think is needed?' and 'How did they think the meeting went?'

The honest answer from staff to some of these questions may be, 'I don't really know' because parents have not been consulted, or only at such a superficial level that genuine views have not emerged. A real effort to find out the views and interests of parents means that they are consulted *before* plans are finalised.

Parents can be asked in what way they would like to be more involved with the setting but they are also experienced 'consumers' of the existing pattern. For instance, parents whose children are settled can be asked for their informed opinion on such issues as the first contact between families and the setting or how the early weeks of their child's attendance could have been eased. Parents' views provide another perspective but do not give a blueprint that has to be followed without further discussion. You would weigh up what parents express through their opinions and look for patterns. The concern or view of just one parent is of value but should usually not shift practice unless it becomes clear that other parents share that opinion or experience. Whatever the pattern, it is important that staff teams work to take disagreement or criticism from parents in a constructive way.

One mother who says 'Nobody was friendly to me when I was settling my child' may have reacted as much to her own discomfort as staff behaviour. Her view is valid and should alert staff that they need to make very definite friendly approaches to put this person at her ease. However, several comments from parents along these lines should be a warning that, whether staff intend it or not, their way of organising the settling-in period for children is not acting as an effective welcome to parents.

Parents' views are an important source of information. Consultation can provide a timely reminder that it does not matter how good your intentions for an activity to involve parents are; the consequences are negative if parents felt unwelcome or that staff had lectured at them in a patronising way.

Meeting parents' genuine preferences may not always be possible, certainly not if they go counter to values in the setting that are non-negotiable. It is important not to raise parents' expectations that any opinions and preferences will be honoured in the setting – any more than staff should expect their suggestions to be applied promptly and in full in parents' own homes.

For instance, good practice in any early years setting should include a practical application of equal opportunities – on gender, ethnic group and culture and disabilities. You could not follow parents' views, however strongly felt, that their boys should be kept away from the cooking activities or that their girls should be dissuaded from using the climbing frame. Nor could you follow any parent's request that their child should not play with other children who differ in ethnic group or religion from the family.

A vital element in partnership will always be to explain to parents at the first meeting (through conversation and written material about your setting) how some aspects of practice are non-negotiable. Further conversation will be necessary if events lead to potential disagreement. When parents and staff hold incompatible views with equal conviction, a discussion will not be easy but can be possible. Honesty, tact and respect for views which you do not share may help to bring about a working acceptance.

Continued open communication between staff and parents can also highlight that they have quite distinct reasons for promoting or joining in activities. Differing motivations are not necessarily a problem so long as they are expressed. However, if they remain as the unspoken hopes and firm assumptions of the adults involved, then misunderstanding and disappointment can follow.

The staff of a nursery or playgroup may have two reasons for encouraging parents to join the group on a regular basis: the hope that parents will understand more about the aims of the setting and that more adult helpers will expand what can be offered to the children. On the other hand, parents who may accept the invitation as a short-term involvement can have differing reasons: some are interested to see how their own child behaves in the group, others would welcome the company of adults and some are pleased to help.

The differing perspectives may not be a difficulty but open communication will be important in making sure that hopes do not go sour. A parent who wants some adult company may not find this wish met in a busy group where adults must have most of their attention on the children. Staff who hope that parents will understand and agree with their methods are probably not taking the most direct and effective route to communication, which would be to have conversations with parents or provide written material that directly addressed the setting's approach to helping children to learn.

Genuine partnership with parents in an early years setting requires thought and that workers address their own assumptions about parents, professionalism and working together. Good communication is also essential to developing and maintaining a working partnership and this topic is addressed in the next chapter.

11

BUILDING RELATIONSHIPS AND GOOD COMMUNICATION

RELATIONSHIPS BETWEEN THE ADULTS

When adults have a group label attached to them, such as ethnic group, gender or social class, it is far too easy to leap to conclusions about individuals because of an overall image assigned to the group. This pattern can happen between adults-as-parents and adults-as-workers in early years. The generalisations may be positive but in times of stress they become negative: 'The parents simply aren't interested!' or 'The staff are an unfriendly bunch of know-alls!' Two related themes which run through this chapter are that:

1) Early years workers sometimes lose sight of the essential fact that parents are people who have children of their own.

Parents have the same mix of personalities and worries as other adults. The same basic rules of communication apply as in other adult relationships, and continue to apply in most part even when adults vary in ethnic group or social class. The parent-staff relationship is a particular kind but it is still a relationship between adults.

In the same way, parents need to remind themselves that:

2) Staff are people who are working with young children and families.

Staff are fellow-adults and the professional status and experience does not mean they do not have feelings too.

Does being professional get in the way?

Early years workers have a package of expertise, knowledge and experience to offer. The term professional is used here to distinguish workers from parents but not to suggest that the expertise of one group is necessarily greater than the other.

Sometimes workers believe that their professional role justifies a one-way view of parent involvement (see the discussion on page 174). In this situation, the professional role can get in the way because workers are assuming that they have the knowledge to advise, or tell, parents how to deal with their children but not that the workers could usefully listen in return. An exclusive sense of shared professional status can lead colleagues to close ranks and believe that only fellow-workers are competent to comment

Friendly relationships will always be central to partnership.

on the work. A centre or school with this atmosphere will not operate in the spirit of partnership because of the staff's unwillingness to share skills or admit ignorance to people who are 'just parents'. All professions have some areas of uncertainty and a distance between practitioners and parents can serve as a protective barrier.

On the other hand, parents can themselves conspire in losing the individual in the child care or educational role, preferring to believe that staff are 100% experts or have a hide like a rhinoceros to deal with hurtful remarks. Parents can choose to relate to the person behind the role label and still maintain a good working relationship.

Staff need to aim for a friendly relationship with parents, but it is still a working relationship. Staff and parents have not come together because they have chosen each other as friends. There may be difficulties to iron out in the difference between a friendly professional and a friend, because it is not appropriate to behave in the same way in the two roles. It is inevitable that you will feel more comfortable with some parents, and they with you. But you have a responsibility to judge priorities in your work and not to have favourites, or enemies, in the parent group.

Bringing expectations to a relationship

Nobody comes cold to any contact with another adult; everyone has expectations about how other adults are likely to react and ways to make sense of behaviour. When there is a role label such as 'parent', 'teacher' or 'centre worker' then adults bring specialised expectations from previous experience or hearsay.

Workers may have built up an image of parents as a group from their training, from the input of colleagues and from generalisations developed from contact with a few individual parents. The image may be relatively positive or more negative and the danger of strong expectations is that experience is then interpreted to fit them. So, a parent who fits the expectations is seen as further proof and one who does not is viewed as an exception. With negative images of parents this might be that 'Of course, Anna's parents are fine but mostly the parents are an awkward bunch.'

Anyone working with children will have some areas of relative ignorance and, especially if their view of a professional is restrictive, may feel threatened by parents' detailed knowledge of child-rearing and expertise about their own child. You need to feel confident about your own contribution to allow for that of others. It is noticeable that, in early years centres where senior workers ensure an effective support system, the staff are far more likely to relate positively to parents. I have certainly known centres where the workers' feelings of low self-esteem, and resentment at their treatment by seniors, have spilled over into dismissive relations with parents.

Parents, in turn, may be affected by memories of their own schooldays, whether the workers with whom they are relating are teachers or not. If the memories are unhappy, then parents are more likely to be suspicious of staff and quick to defend themselves and their child against criticism. If the memories are happy then relations may be easier, although parents have to find and develop an adult relationship with staff. They are no longer the child in this situation and may have to acknowledge mixed feelings as they balance a wish to be cooperative with the importance of supporting and, if necessary, speaking up strongly for their child.

Parents who have continuing difficulties with authority in various guises may view early years workers as another example of 'them'. You have to recognise and understand this perspective; it is not fair but parents will take time to make you an exception to their general rule. Parents and workers share the responsibility for distinguishing this adult relationship from others in which they have had problems.

Making sense of others' behaviour

'Parent' and 'worker' are roles that adults fulfil. Their behaviour follows the general rules for any adults; neither group is some special breed. An important guideline is that it is risky to generalise from people's behaviour to what they are like as individuals or their intentions towards you. You can observe behaviour; the rest is guesswork. It is especially important to recall this point when the role taken by an adult is likely to shape your interpretations.

Differences in ethnic group and cultural difference may lead to individual differences in perspective but it is just as likely that you will have common ground as much as variation, especially in a shared commitment to the children. Certainly it is not justifiable to view an ethnic difference between two disagreeing parties as evidence that at least one person is motivated by racism. The difference is not sufficient reason without further patterns of behaviour.

You cannot come to any fair conclusions without a reasonable sample of behaviour – the same point made within chapter 3 on observation of children. For instance, the beginning and end of a day or session are not usually typical of the rest of the time and staff would be unhappy about having all their work judged on what can be busy, sometimes fairly chaotic, transition times. So, early years workers cannot judge parents and their interest in their children on this very small sample of behaviour. Children often play up at going home time and a parent may lose patience, trying yet again to get outdoor clothes on an uncooperative small body, and with an audience. This event is not necessarily typical of this child, the parent and the time they spend together outside your setting. Parents might just as unreasonably conclude that their children spend their day bored or out of control and so they go wild on leaving.

Parents are interested in their children

Some workers point to low attendance by parents at particular activities arranged by the setting as evidence that parents are not interested in their own children. This is an unreasonable conclusion. Parents may not attend activities for a number of reasons other than lack of interest in their own children. They may have limited free time from other responsibilities, they may not share a first language with staff and they may lack sitters for evening meetings or the activities may not be about issues that parents regard as high priority.

Parents can be involved with and intensely interested in their own children without necessarily sharing identical values and approaches as early years workers. There are different routes for ensuring that children develop and learn and other forums for play and learning in addition to the child-centred nature of most early years settings.

So, a high level of attendance is neither the only, nor necessarily the best measure of parents' interest in the children and how they progress in your setting. A low level of attendance may be a measure of a setting's failure so far to communicate clearly with parents and listen to their views. Workers would, for example, be ready to defend themselves if a parent claimed that those workers were uninterested in the parent's child because the parent had rarely seen the worker talking with that child. Again, fair judgements depend on obtaining a representative sample of behaviour and on allowing for other explanations besides what seems to be the obvious one.

Parents are already involved with their children

Some discussions of partnership give the impression that getting parents involved in the early years setting is the only way to encourage them to become appropriately involved in their children's lives. Yet, all parents are involved with their children in a way that directly affects those children's future lives. For good or ill, parents are a formative influence on their children. Many parents are positively involved with their children in ways that directly encourage the children's learning.

Some staff working with children underestimate or simply have no knowledge of what parents have done and are still undertaking with their children at home. The gap in their understanding is ironic given the common view from workers that parents underestimate what is achieved within early years settings and school. The limited knowledge and mutual awareness is not surprising given the restricted opportunities for conversation during a normal day.

Being involved and being consulted

Wishing to be involved in the activities of an early years centre and wanting to be consulted about the centre or one's own children are two separate, although overlapping areas.

Some parents, for a variety of reasons, are pleased to take up invitations that offer closer involvement in daily activities of a centre, give opportunities for social contact with workers and other parents or attend meetings. Some parents choose not to become involved, especially when time and physical presence during the day is required, but wish to be consulted. This consultation may be about their own child(ren), so that they as parents are a full part of any decision made. Some parents also wish to have their opinion asked about issues relevant to the running of the nursery or playgroup.

Few parents want to take over a nursery or playgroup, although some managers and team leaders fear that parents on management committees or similar bodies will inevitably cause this type of disruption. Most parents do not want to devote their limited time and energy to the time-consuming task of running an early years centre. However, many appreciate being consulted.

Parents' and workers' perspectives should be different

It is sometimes said that parents see an early years centre through the needs of their own child(ren) and that workers take a broader view. This comment is accurate and fair unless the comment on parents' perspective is a criticism, that parents take a narrow, subjective view of a centre or service. Children need both adults who will champion them as individuals and those who will look to the well-being of the whole group. Both are necessary and important roles, not necessarily in competition and both are equally legitimate. With an opportunity for conversation, seasoned with a respect for each other's position, workers and parents could see more through each other's eyes.

Despite the advances in recognition of the importance of the early years, workers can still experience a broad social view that working with young children, especially outside the context of a school is less important and/or an easy job anyone could do. When professional status is insecure, there can sometimes be a restrictive sense of professionalism in self-defence. Ironically, the undervaluing of time and expertise with young children is an experience common to parents and workers alike; the experience could bring people together. Within any early years setting senior staff have an important role to play in helping staff to value their own skills and experience but not at the cost of down-playing the expertise of parents. Confidence in what you have to offer will be an essential basis genuinely to value and welcome the contribution of the parents. It seems possible that the more positive profile of early years facilities, especially of pre-school education, has had the unfortunate side-effect of further downgrading the great potential for children to learn in their own home (see comments on page 65).

A blend of the different and equally valid perspectives of both staff and parents will build a positive environment in which children can grow and develop. The less each side understands, or tries to understand, each other, the more likely there is to be misunderstandings and perhaps hostilities, which will not ease children's lives.

Good communication

All activities that bring parents and workers together, however briefly, demand the skills appropriate to contact and communication between adults. You will already be aware of these skills, to some extent. However, it is easier to be aware of poor people skills when you are on the receiving end than to realise and accept that your own communications could be improved. For example, most people are swifter to notice that someone is not listening to them than to realise that they themselves are failing to listen properly.

The relationship between workers and parents is between adults so all that follows in this section is potentially relevant to both groups. The discussion is written to workers partly because you are the most likely readers of this book, but also because the conversations will be taking place in your setting. You are being employed to work well with children and parents, you and your colleagues set the atmosphere in the centre and so it is appropriate that the primary responsibility rests with you to build on your skills and work for positive communication with parents.

Learning to listen well

Some people are said to be natural, good listeners but everyone can learn to listen well. Firstly, you need to be aware of the barriers to listening effectively. You can make changes in your way of communicating, if you are motivated to do so. You will not listen well when:

- You want to hear a particular message, probably one that agrees with your own view, and you listen selectively for that.
- You are busy planning or worrying about what you are going to say next and not listening to what the other person is telling you now.
- You are simply marking time until you can resume talking yourself.
- You have little or no respect for the other person. You will then dismiss any value in what she or he says.
- There are physical problems for listening: the setting is noisy, you have a bad headache or neither of you can stand or sit comfortably in the cramped setting.
- An additional feature of working with young children is that you are trying to listen at the same time as having responsibility for the children and this leads to distraction and interruption.

Developing active listening
Real listening takes energy because you are concentrating on what other people are saying, both their words and how they say them. Active listening, which is crucial when you are talking with parents, especially when there is some difficulty, means putting on one side your own views and what you want to say or ask. You are offering the other person the respect of your time and attention.

Several practical points arise in early years centres:

- Look at how your setting may affect your ability to listen well and how much you could rearrange furniture, for instance.
- You need a practical approach to dealing with interruptions and minor crises. You might excuse yourself from conversation with a parent in order to deal briefly with the children, perhaps with a, 'Please excuse me for a moment' and then easing back into the conversation with, 'You were telling me about . . .'
- A balance has to be held between time for parents and time for children. Certainly, workers who have full responsibility for a group of children cannot switch attention fully to a parent for long periods of time, however pressing that parent's need may appear. Discuss within your team and with senior workers how best to handle this situation – perhaps it will be possible to offer a time and place to talk later in the day or offer to a parent that he or she could talk with a senior worker.

- If your listening is in the special context of offering counselling help to another adult then you should both be somewhere quiet and away from the children.

How you sit and stand in conversation with another adult can make a double contribution to good listening: in helping you to listen better and in communicating to the other person, in a way as loud as words, that he or she has your full attention.

- Face the other person squarely, so you can see her or him clearly and are not distracted.
- It is encouraging to the other person if your posture is open and relaxed, yet attentive. Firmly crossed arms, for instance, tend to look like a barrier.
- Lean forward slightly towards the other person – rather than being bolt upright or appearing to lean away. Respect what seems to be a comfortable distance for the other person.
- Make regular eye contact with the other person but do not hold a long stare – this usually makes people uncomfortable. Again, be guided by the amount of eye contact that seems comfortable for the other person.

Overall you are aiming for a sitting or standing posture that looks and feels attentive but not intimidating.

The power of body language

A considerable proportion of the total message you receive from another adult in a face-to-face conversation comes from the non-verbal sources of communication, especially from facial expression and the eyes. Everyone receives and acts upon these unspoken messages and other people are, of course, reacting to your non-verbal communication. In face-to-face exchanges, you cannot stop yourself communicating through your expression and body posture, nor should you try. However, your communication can be more effective if you become aware of the non-verbal side.

All early years workers need to be aware of their body language, as much for your work with the children as communication with parents. You can tune yourself into non-verbal communication by taking note of the internal messages of your body. Perhaps you feel yourself knotting up inside as you approach a conversation with an adult with whom you find it hard to relate. Unless you listen to what your body is telling you and consciously relax, the tension will show through stiff posture or a clipped edge to your voice. The discomfort will also inhibit your listening.

Unless you have the opportunity to watch yourself on video, you will only have a limited sense of your non-verbal habits. A good working relationship between colleagues can allow feedback on each other's body language. Perhaps you notice that your colleague tends to look away from the other person when she is about to broach an issue about which she has very strong feelings. In her turn, your colleague might alert you to your habit of coughing in a nervous way when someone asks you a question on which you are uncertain.

Your communication with others will improve as you become more aware of the non-verbal as well as the verbal aspects. It is equally important that you are aware of the conclusions you draw from the body language of others. You may need to pin down the source of a gut feeling about a parent since it may be less what was said than how. Additionally, most people are especially influenced, or irritated by, certain gestures or facial expressions and it is useful to get these in perspective as your personal raw spot and not to over-generalise.

There are individual differences in body language, although some patterns are influenced by cultural traditions and learned in much the same way as patterns of expression in spoken language. As an early years worker it is important to be aware of broad differences between cultures such as: relative differences in how close people tend to stand to one another, using touch to emphasise a point, the expressiveness of gestures or the extent of eye contact. But you will not be able to work along firm generalisations since there is as much variety within cultures as between.

It is possible to become overly conscious of non-verbal communication when you first become aware of this channel for messages. With practice and a willingness to view body language as helpful rather than alarming, any heightened awareness will settle down into a useful sensitivity to yourself and others.

Use of words

Every profession has some shared professional language and early years is no exception. You might well realise that phrases such as 'fine physical coordination' or 'socio-emotional development' are not in everyday use outside early years settings. You do not have to speak to parents slowly in words of one syllable but professional phrases deserve explanation through practical example, such as, 'how Andrea manages to pour water' or 'how Jamal plays with other children'. Sometimes, you may not anticipate the possible confusions from what seem like everyday phrases to you but actually have professional meanings. Parents new to an early years setting may have doubts about how their child will 'learn through play' or think that 'creative activities' will just be closely supervised drawing.

You might like to listen in to yourself and colleagues and pick out the shared early years language. Think and discuss how you can reword what you say, but not appear patronising to parents – who may, of course, be equally able to baffle you with specialised terms from their own area of work or interests.

Opinions and suggestions

The skills of expressing opinions were discussed on page 18 in the context of sharing records and observations with parents. These skills are important in the broader context of conversations with parents.

There is no way that you can ensure that someone never takes offence, any more than you could make sure that you never felt uneasy or threatened. But there are positive guidelines that increase the chance that parents, or colleagues with whom you are having a difficult conversation, will listen rather than go on the defensive. If you take the lead in being positive and constructive, it is more likely that parents (or colleagues) may follow your lead.

- If you are expressing an opinion then give it honestly as a personal view, as 'I think that . . .' or 'I feel that . . .' The person on the receiving end may still wish to argue but you have more chance of a conversation than the heavy-footed approach of, 'We all think that . . .' (when this is not a group consensus) or 'It's obvious that . . .'
- You can give feedback on your experience of what somebody has done or not done and your feelings about it. But this example neither gives the right to generalise about another adult's behaviour in other situations nor to make judgements on their personality. Consider how differently you might feel if a parent made comment (a) or (b) to you:
    - (a) I didn't feel welcome when I was settling Jamie in because nobody said "Hello" to me.'
    - (b) 'You staff are a stuck-up, unfriendly bunch.'
- Nobody is a 100% expert but it can be tempting to pronounce sometimes as if one were. Yet, other adults are more likely to benefit from your genuine expertise if you offer a clear suggestion that they can turn over in their mind. You could offer, 'Have you considered . . .?' or 'I'm wondering if you are overlooking . . . . about Megan's behaviour'. Such an approach is also more respectful than the shutting down of, 'If only you hadn't . . .' or 'Well, if you will insist on . . .'
- You have experience to share (with colleagues as well as parents) but this can be undermining if it is given as straight criticism. You will, for instance, support a parent-helper better by saying, 'I find the children stay more absorbed in the story when I turn the book towards them' than the blunt, 'That's the wrong way to read to a group of children'.
- You may be quick to say that other adults make more effort to complain than to compliment but be aware also of your own behaviour. You can model a positive approach by putting at least as much effort into communicating encouragement and praise as on expressing what has concerned or irritated you. A difficulty in increasing compliments can be that some adults find it hard to accept them graciously. Again, you can model a welcoming reaction. For instance, if a parent says, 'Thanks for listening to me yesterday', you can reply with a positive, 'You're welcome', rather than a self-deprecating, 'That's all right. I'm not sure I was much help anyway.'

When you are on the receiving end of suggestions and opinions, it is possible to learn for the future. Feedback will not improve your practice if you take it as a source of regretful 'if only's about the past. You can, of course, invite comments from others, colleagues perhaps. You need to listen carefully to what is said and check that you have understood what the other person is telling you. You may feel initially in agreement, or inclined to argue. Hold back for the moment and make sure that you are grasping what is being said, since there may be useful feedback even if perhaps it is not well expressed. You can turn over in your mind what has been suggested and perhaps compare this view with what other people may have said before. If it makes sense to adjust your approach, you can make small changes over time.

Dealing with serious disagreements

There is no magical solution to dealing with anger from other adults but some approaches are more positive than others. The following suggestions can help to prevent minor disagreements blowing up into full-scale rows and to divert angry expressions in your centre.

Making sense of how anger arises
The anger, or irritation of another adult often feels like a personal attack but it is unhelpful to see this emotion solely in this way. This perspective is not excusing the behaviour but is seeking a broader perspective.

Anger is the tip of a some very different emotional icebergs.

- Sometimes another adult may be angry specifically with you – perhaps with good reason.
- If a setting does not allow parents easy conversational access to workers, then a resolvable issue can reach boiling point before normally reasonable parents grit their teeth to say, 'Enough is enough!'
- Some adults' anger is a reflection of low self-esteem. It is easier – not necessarily as a conscious process – to find continuous fault with others than to take a realistic look at their own life.
- Some adults have learned to use anger, even over minor issues, as a way of showing strength and individuality. The emotion can also be an effective way of keeping others at a distance. The behaviour looks strong, even intimidating, but is actually a sign of weakness.
- Sometimes, as unlikely as it can feel on the receiving end, anger is a plea for help.
- Sometimes, anger will be deflected onto you in the setting because you are available, unlike the true source of a parent's frustration: the buses, the housing department or a miserable family situation.

If you can be honest with yourself, you will undoubtedly have behaved in some of the ways above within your life at some time.

Your feelings and reactions

You need to get in touch with how you personally react to anger from another adult. Some people feel reasonably able to cope calmly, some are very anxious, some have to work hard not to return anger with even more anger. You need to be aware of your own likely reactions, to accept them but not let them hinder a positive approach. Whether you like it or not, your body will react if you feel under attack: your heart rate increases, your breathing will get faster and more shallow and you may perspire. This is the flight or fight automatic reaction that we share with the rest of the animal kingdom. Try to view this positively by seeing the physical reactions as preparation, say to yourself, 'I'm ready'. If you view the physical changes negatively then it can sap your energy to deal with the immediate situation, feeling, 'On top of everything else, I've got sweaty palms!'

Catching anger early

Some angry incidents, not all, are potentially avoidable. Good communication skills make a great difference in encouraging conversation rather than argument. (Look back at 'Opinions and suggestions' on page 193.) A welcoming atmosphere in an early years setting and a respectful approach to parents will also ensure that fair-minded adults are not driven towards extreme reactions through being dismissed as 'just parents'. It is also possible to take control of your own behaviour so that incidents do not become worse.

Dealing with an angry adult

Many early years workers have skills for dealing with the anger of others; you apply them in handling children. The skills are similar in tense communication with adults.

- A key point is to stay calm. If you answer anger with more anger then an incident will worsen quickly, leaving your control.
- Show the other adult that you recognise the strong feelings and are ready to listen: 'I can see you're angry. Please tell me what has happened.' Do not try to work out whether the anger is justified; find out why this person is angry. Let them talk and show that you are listening (see the points about active listening on page 190).
- Recognise that whatever you say will be filtered through the anger until the other person calms. So, keep what you say simple and to the point. When adults are angry, they are not responsive to logical argument and you have to be cautious with questions, certainly 'Why?' questions that can sound confrontational.
- If there is a quick and appropriate solution, then offer it. If apologies are due, then say 'Sorry' without lots of self-justification and find out how to avoid this mistake or oversight in the future. However, it is not wise to use an apology just to stop the conversation.
- Listen carefully to what a parent is saying but check on the facts before taking any action. For instance, you should not take a furious parent's word as the only evidence that named children are guilty of, for instance, bullying this parent's child.

Dealing with the aftermath

In your job, an emotionally charged incident will have a tomorrow and someone – most likely you – needs to ensure that the relationship is re-established. It will not be helpful to pretend that an angry exchange never happened. Relations need to be taken on from, 'Things seemed to get out of hand on Tuesday. I'd like to talk it over with you.' The answer may be 'No' but then you have shown willing. Quite often an angry person, parent or colleague, is embarrassed, maybe upset and finding it hard to apologise. 'Tomorrow' is not the time to get angry in your turn, although sometimes it can be the opportunity for you to express feelings of shock or confusion about the incident. You need to create a constructive conversation in which there can be explanations, information-gathering and any plans for the future.

You cannot directly control the behaviour of other people but what you do becomes a factor in any situation. If you are prepared to try different approaches to dealing with the anger of others, you may be pleasantly surprised by your growing ability to cope with situations which previously you dreaded or which quickly became shouting matches. (Look also in the suggested reading on page 201 for references on an assertive approach.)

Be prepared to reflect on an incident later. If you are satisfied with how you handled it, then be pleased for yourself and your skills. If you feel matters could have gone better, then what have you learned for the future? More fraught situations may leave you in need of support yourself from colleagues or a senior worker in your setting.

Being professional

You can decide in your personal life whether or not to take this positive approach to anger; if you choose to have a row in a shop that is your business. However, in professional life more is appropriately expected of you in patience, self-restraint and understanding the perspective of others. In this sense, the work role limits you to an acceptable range of responses.

However, holding a post in an early years setting should not doom you to becoming a verbal, or physical, punchbag. It is appropriate to set limits and these can be communicated assertively and not with aggression. By spoken word and assertive body language you can often take control of a situation. You might say, 'I can see that you're angry. I'm willing to listen, but I'm not going to stand here and have you swear at me' or 'Your shouting is upsetting the children. I'll talk with you in the hallway, not here.' There may be times when you need to walk away or firmly accompany another adult out of the room.

Good communication skills and an assertive approach should enable you to handle and defuse many incidents. However, some early years workers have jobs that bring them into contact with adults under extreme stress or those who have learned to cope with any frustrations through aggression. Any parents who have an alcohol or drug dependence problem may also be unpredictable. Under such circumstances you must know how to summon help swiftly from colleagues or from the police. It is good practice to seek support when an incident is moving beyond the skills of one person to cope or is potentially dangerous to the children.

HELPING ADULTS WITH PROBLEMS

Parents may sometimes ask for your opinion or advice. If you work in a setting where parents have complex and long-term problems in their lives, then the prospect of helping can be daunting.

In some settings, early years workers will need the specific skills of counselling which have to be gained through attendance on a relevant course and supervised practice. Genuine helping through the counselling process is about aiding other adults to understand their difficulties in ways that enable them to tackle those problems or learn to live with situations that they cannot really change. Counselling is not advice giving, nor heavy-handed interpretations of people's feelings or behaviour. A good counsellor spends time listening and working to understand the other person's perspective. Counsellors do not tell people what to do but they support others in considering options and coming to a realistic judgement of what could be possible.

Many early years workers have a pattern of job responsibilities that leave time only for short conversations with parents. However, even a brief conversation will be more helpful to a parent if you listen and discuss rather than tell. This section is written for you. If you are interested in reading more about the counselling process you will find suggestions on page 201.

Avoid giving quick solutions

When other adults come to you with a difficulty or dilemma, you may be tempted to offer your ideas about what they could do as soon as you have heard a brief outline of the problem. Quite often, the other person may be pressing you for a quick answer. Falling in with this is risky on several counts:

- You have not had time really to understand the problem as this person is experiencing it. The danger is that you will have to make sense of the difficulty by assuming it is very similar to an experience of your own or to that of another parent. But, the situations may be very different, for instance, of two parents who ask for advice on getting their children to bed or with waking babies. What helped one parent may not be suitable or possible for another.
- Whenever a person's difficult experiences are slotted into a box – 'just like Ben's problem,' or 'typical worrying young Mum' – you are effectively saying to this

individual that 'Your problem isn't that important; I've seen it all before'. Such a reaction is disrespectful.

● Whenever you put yourself in the role of expert on a problem (and perhaps the parent is pushing you hard in this direction) you run the risk of taking responsibility for the situation. If your quick solution works, then the other adult has not learned that she or he can cope, because the suggestion was yours, not an idea reached jointly. If the solution fails or backfires in some way, then it will be your fault.

Listen to what is being said

However hard other adults push you to, 'Tell me what I should do', ask them to tell you about what they are experiencing and listen carefully to what they say and how it is said. To be of any real help, you need to see the situation through their eyes: what is happening at the moment, what they have tried, what they feel is possible or impossible. This will not necessarily be a long conversation but giving time to listen shows that you take the other person and their concerns seriously.

All the points on page 190 about active listening apply here. You will be talking sometimes, as well as listening, but what you say needs to encourage the other adult to talk in their own way. It is not useful to cross-question people and open-ended questions of 'What?' and 'How?' are usually better than closed ones. You need to ensure that you understand what the other person is saying and this can be achieved through summarising what you have heard in your own words – 'If I've got it right, you feel that. . . .' This attempt to understand is far more helpful than imposing your own view with, 'You clearly have a problem about. . . .'

Talk through any suggestions

A single, 'I think you ought to . . .' is not generally helpful. You need to talk around several possibilities with the other person, or at the very least have an open discussion about how this person could best put into practice a general approach that has worked for others. It is sometimes useful to explore what the other person has already tried and not necessarily to abandon an idea that did not work for them. Perhaps this person did not understand the approach or might now be able to put the necessary amount of effort into changing the situation. An experience of failure will mean that the other person is unlikely to try a similar approach unless you talk through with them what will probably make it work this time.

A helpful conversation covers what could support other people or get in the way as he or she tries to face and cope with the difficulty. In the end it will be their decision about any course of action, including none at all. You may feel frustrated by their inaction but it is the other person's choice and if you do not become irritated then the door is open for conversation in the future.

Respect confidentiality

Even if they do not specifically ask you, most people expect that personal conversations about problems will remain confidential. This expectation is fair and should be respected. Parents' personal experiences or problems should not be the source of gossip among staff and certainly not repeated to other parents or outside the setting.

It is appropriate that workers on the same staff team exchange information in order to be of most help. In a busy early years setting you have to be alert that you do not hold conversations with colleagues, that are appropriate between the two of you, but are taking place within earshot of the children or parents. Sometimes parents themselves may start to talk in the hearing of children, perhaps their own child with whom they have the difficulty. You should move the conversation to somewhere more private or suggest that the parent make an appointment to talk later.

Respect for confidentiality may present you with a dilemma. Suppose that a parent talks about something that you know you must pass on, for instance, that the parent or a partner is hitting the child who is already on the child protection register. The parent says, 'This is just between you and me'. Knowing that you must pass on this information, you have two choices:

- Suppose you allow the parents to carry on because you think she may stop talking otherwise. The consequence of this option is that you are being dishonest. The parent will discover you have broken confidence and is far less likely to trust you, or other professionals, in the future.
- The other choice is to be honest and say, 'If you tell me more about . . . then I have to pass it on to my manager.' The consequence then is that the other person makes an informed choice about whether to continue talking, to stop or maybe to return to talk later.

Good practice has to be the second alternative and the introductory material about your setting should make clear to parents that the team shares information in a respectful way and cannot promise to keep family secrets that threaten a child's welfare.

Remember this is not your problem

The cliché is that 'a problem shared is a problem halved'. Unfortunately, without a grasp of basic helping skills, adults can find that listening to the difficulties and worries of another adult had led to two people feeling weighed down by the same problem. Being truly helpful means a delicate balance between caring enough to offer your time and effort while keeping a sense of detachment. You should neither take responsibility for nor feel overwhelmed by the problems of a parent, or a colleague. Again, within any early years setting there should be the opportunity to talk with a colleague, perhaps a senior worker who gives you supervision, and to work through those times when you feel too closely involved with another person's dilemmas.

Be realistic about what is possible

Finally, do not burden yourself with unrealistically high expectations. Even counsellors who spend many sessions with a client sometimes feel that they have made only limited progress. So do not expect to resolve complex adult problems in a couple of short conversations. Ideally, any early years setting should have someone, perhaps a senior worker, who can give time and skills for difficulties that cannot be explored in short conversations.

POSITIVE RELATIONSHIPS WITH PARENTS

Several, related themes have run through this chapter.

- The importance of looking, at least sometimes, through the parents' eyes and appreciating their perspective, which may well differ from your own and that of colleagues. You do not have to agree with parents' opinions and priorities but communication with your setting will be greatly improved if you have a grasp of how parents view the setting and their hopes and expectations. Their priorities may not be yours but children's experience in your centre will be improved if you allow for families' viewpoints.
- Working well with other adults inevitably leads you to look at yourself, your own package of strengths and weaker points. Good practice has to include the willingness to continue to learn and to make some changes.
- Early years workers need to take responsibility for their own behaviour and the consequences of their actions. For instance, a view that 'Parents are the visitors here. They should say, "Hello" first, not us' is a refusal to share the effort in making a good working relationship. One could just as easily claim that workers are comfortable on their own territory; they should make the moves to put parents at ease. You will find some parents harder to work with than others but again a view that, 'She makes me feel small. It's her fault we don't get along' is making the other person responsible not only for their behaviour but also for your feelings. You cannot directly control their behaviour, but you could try a different approach to her and work on your feelings about feeling 'small'.

Working towards good relationships with parents is not always easy but then relationships between adults usually require some time, effort and commitment. Parents are people and staff are people and, although the relationship is of a particular kind, workers are in deep trouble if they forget that they share an adult status with parents. Your skills for dealing with fellow-adults need to be sharpened; you are not dealing with a different species.

SUGGESTED FURTHER READING

Back, Ken and Kate with Bates, Terry (1991) *Assertiveness at Work – A Practical Guide to Handling Awkward Situations*. McGraw–Hill.

Culley, Sue (1991) *Integrative Counselling Skills in Action*. Sage.

Kerr, Susan (1993) *Your Child with Special Needs*. Hodder & Stoughton.

Lindon, Jennie and Lance (1993) *Your Child from 5–11*. Hodder & Stoughton.

Lindon, Jennie and Lance (1997) *Working Together for Young Children: A Guide for Managers and Staff*. Macmillan.

Murgartroyd, Stephen (1985) *Counselling and Helping*. British Psychological Society/Methuen.

Pugh, Gillian and De'Ath, Erica (1989) *Working Towards Partnership in the Early Years*. National Children's Bureau.

Tizard, Barbara, Mortimore, Jo and Burchell, Bebb (1981) *Involving Parents in Nursery and Infant Schools*. Grant McIntyre.

INDEX